"Daman carefully demonstrates from Scripture and his own pastoral experience that the weeping shepherd reflects the heart of Christ by entering into the sorrows, grief, and pain of the sheep entrusted to his care. I was reminded that a pastor must never be detached or indifferent but that he will suffer, and yet at the same time he must keep a proper perspective. I was profoundly moved and inspired by this book and heartily encourage every pastor to read it."

Les Lofquist, Executive Director,
IFCA International

"This book lucidly describes the struggle of so many in ministry. Daman does another admirable job of developing the issues in ministry that bring us to the brink of 'throwing in the towel.' But he doesn't leave it there; he goes on to give us the all-important biblical answers that aid us in faithfully staying on track. This is a must read for all in ministry."

Michael Jones, Assistant Director,
Village Missions

"Daman has done a wonderful job of allowing those of us in ministry to open up to our feelings of hurt and pain when we are rejected, and he helps us face into the reality of loss when we are wounded and thrown out of a place of ministry! Not only does Daman speak clearly and graciously, he helps us gain biblical perspective by taking us to God's Word for healing and insight! Good job, Glenn!"

Patrick A. Blewett, Dean,
A. W. Tozer Theological Seminary

"After over three decades of pastoral ministry, Daman understands the depth of anguish its difficulties can bring. In this book he carefully develops the scriptural perspectives that make it possible for pastors to experience the joy of the Lord no matter how difficult ministry sometimes becomes. Pastors who feel under attack by those they seek to serve, or have survived such attacks, will profit from reading it."

Earl Brubaker, Former Executive Director,
Northwest Independent Church Extension

"Daman's pastoral care comes through to those feeling burned out, ill-equipped, and bitter towards God and ministry. By allowing our viewpoints on pastoral ministry to be challenged and changed by engaging with biblical examples of suffering such as we find in Job, Daman releases in us the care and vulnerability to experience the pain of ministry with courage and health. This is a must-read for every pastor—and for all who aspire to the noble work of a shepherd."

Kevin Yeadon,
Chi Alpha Campus Ministries

GLENN C. DAMAN

WHEN SHEPHERDS WEEP

Finding Tears of Joy for Wounded Pastors

LEXHAM PRESS

To Emily and Paige.
They are a wonderful addition to our family
and a true blessing and joy.

To the people of River Christian Church, Wibaux Bible Church,
and Cascade Locks Community Church. Throughout all the ups and
downs and struggles of ministry they have been supportive of my ministry,
gracious with my failures, and patient with my shortcomings.

Contents

Foreword

My friendship with Glenn began when we met in Ted Stevens Anchorage International Airport. Glenn hailed me as he descended the escalator and we went to claim our baggage. Over the next week we visited schools, individuals, and churches in rural areas of Alaska. While we had made acquaintance previously through Village Missions, on this trip I came to appreciate Glenn as a servant of Christ committed to the small church.

Over the intervening years we've each stayed in the other's homes. I came to know his wife, Becky, and their sons, and he made acquaintance with my family. Each of us contributed to the other's writing. My ministry opened the door of friendship with his mother, brothers, and sister. Glenn comes from a rural farming background and a family that is committed to the Lord's work in the local church. The call to ministry that he pursues comes not from family expectation, economic expedience, or academic aptitude but from the voice of the Spirit of Christ summoning him from a northern Idaho farm to his current ministry as a pastor. From our first acquaintance I have always found Glenn to be an easygoing, affable, insightful, and caring person. His books and research have been a great help to me and those with whom I have worked in Village Missions.

Over fifteen years ago Paul Borden began a successful project to improve the quality of leadership for Growing Healthy Churches (formerly American Baptist Churches of the West). Part of the project was to resource pastors with the knowledge of leadership that would equip them as leaders: "We wanted pastors to know how leaders functioned and behaved, and that one of their primary tasks is to disciple and develop new leaders."[1] Borden identified the nature of leadership and the skill sets needed for successful leadership.

Borden is not the only one to train successful leaders for the church. In spite of almost a quarter of a century of intensive efforts to equip leaders, the average pastor has a tenure of only 3.6 years at any place of ministry, and over 60 percent of those entering the ministry today will leave before completing a career. Apparently biblical knowledge and leadership skills alone do not sufficiently found long-term pastoral leadership. In addition there is a trail of blood and tears that marks this exodus. Working as a rural pastor and with rural pastors I have experienced this personally and know individuals who have left the ministry never to return to the church because the pain is so great.

After one has read all the books and taken all the courses there remains an element of ministry required for one to endure and remain faithful to the needs of the body of Christ for the long term. The single greatest predictor of health and success for the local body of Christ remains a faithful, long-term pastoral leadership. This book presents that element: *perspective*. Pain and suffering inevitably accompany ministry. Pain and suffering in Christian ministry remain the barriers to the faithful shepherding the church so desperately needs from its pastor. Glenn does not deny this reality. He acknowledges the necessity of suffering and pain in ministry. He proposes a change in perspective on suffering in ministry, a point of view that allows one to endure and even embrace this difficult part of every ministry.

But this is not Pollyanna. One doesn't merely recite the mantra of Romans 8:28 three times and move ahead in ministry. Glenn has endured his own pain and suffering over his years of ministry. From the crucible of his own experience he faces the deep challenge of enduring faith and enduring faithfulness in ministry. Thorough biblical research undergirds Glenn's recommendations for developing a long-term ministry in the local church. It is a theological examination of one's self, ministry,

---

[1]   Paul D. Borden, *Hit the Bullseye: How Denominations Can Aim Congregations at the Mission Field* (Nashville: Abingdon, 2003), 50.

call, and future that recommends a renewed perspective as a means to long-term ministry.

In one particularly painful time in my ministry career, I was on the brink of leaving the pastorate. My wife and I took time away from our rural church to go to a mall in a nearby city. We sat in crowded anonymity reflecting on what God was doing. Though we had not read Glenn's insights (they had not even been written), we began to experience from our Lord that transformation of perspective about which Glenn writes. We stuck it out. In my years of ministry I have endured deaths, family failure, child molesters in the church, community rejection, leader mutiny, and more. In addition I have worked with some who have endured far more. After thirty-seven-plus years of ministry, I can tell you that this element of perspective in a time of crisis is what most of us who open this book need in order to endure.

Read on. In this book you will find articulated what those in ministry need in order to survive the pain, to suffer and yet to endure. The pain and suffering of ministry in the church are certain. Yet even so, what we need developed further in our lives, and what this book seeks to fortify, is the perspective of faith.

Dr. Vernal Wilkinson
Village Missions, District Representative
Author, *The Bible, Live: A Basic Guide for Preachers
and Teachers in Small Churches*

Preface

Paul knew the pain of ministry. In 2 Corinthians 4 and 5, he piles adjective upon adjective to describe the experiences he faced. He describes being "afflicted," "perplexed," "struck down," "carrying about in the body the dying of Jesus," "being delivered over to death," having death working in him, and the outer man decaying. Twice he mentions his groanings as the pressures of life and ministry burdened him. No matter how broken and defeated we feel because of the circumstances we face in ministry, Paul would be able to fully identify with us. Yet in the same context he states that he also was being renew inwardly day by day and that the in the end he considered all the struggles to be momentary and light as he kept his focus upon the glory that was in store for him.

But here is where we struggle with Paul's words. What he considered to be light and momentary, we find to be overwhelming and debilitating. How then can we change our perspective? How do we learn to view the struggles we face as merely a bump in the road of our journey of ministry?

In this short book we will seek to start a journey of discovery to find out the basis of joy that transcends all the turmoil, discouragements, and struggles of ministry. The purpose of this book is not to provide all the answers to the questions and challenges we face in ministry. There is only one book that can do that, and it was already written two thousand years ago. Rather, the purpose of this book is to point us back to the Bible in our search for meaning, understanding, and perspective. My desire is that this book will serve as a guide to point the reader in the right direction for the answers.

As we seek answers and perspective, in the first two chapters we will overview the various struggles pastors and other church leaders encounter in ministry and how they exact a spiritual and emotional toll upon our families and us. But the purpose of this overview is not to address every problem we face but to cause us to pause and come to grips with the personal pain we experience. As an understanding friend the author wishes to commiserate with you in the opening chapters because like you, I too have suffered and struggled and wanted at times to quit. Too often we strive to deny, conceal, and ignore the inward pain we feel. The result is disastrous. The first step towards spiritual and emotional health is to acknowledge the problem.

In the chapter 3 we will begin to realign our perspective by taking a journey through the biblical teaching regarding God's purpose behind suffering. In the orchestration of God's sovereign will, nothing happens arbitrarily or haphazardly. All things have a purpose and that purpose is ultimately for our good, the growth of the church, and the glory of God.

But this brings us to our understanding of God, which we will examine in chapter 4. Ultimately in the crucible of ministry we need a proper view of God and his working in our life. The irony is that in the midst of serving God, we can lose sight of him. Ministry requires faith, not just faith in the redemptive work of God, but also faith that God can be trusted even when we do not fully understand.

The journey to spiritual health also requires that we have a right understanding of ourselves. One of the reasons we struggle in ministry is because we have a distorted view of what we have been called to be and do. In order for us to have a right perspective of ministry, we must understand who we are in Christ and the implications it has for our ministry. In chapter 5 we take a brief overview of the biblical perspective of our identity in Christ as his servants and the implications it has for ministry.

Ministry also distorts our view of people. As we live in the caldron of ministry we can easily become cynical about the very people we serve. To keep ourselves in balance we must learn to see people through the eyes of Christ. So in chapter 6 we will examine how Scripture provides the foundation for how we see people.

Last, God did not call us to live defeated and discouraged. The Christian life, and ministry, is a call to joy. Thus we examine in chapter 7 the desired result of our study, which is not that we would merely survive in ministry, but that we would thrive and embrace our calling with joy. Ministry is the greatest privilege God gives to us. To be one of his servants is not a curse but a blessing. To complete the journey of developing a right perspective we need to come to the place where we enjoy serving Christ even in the face of the tremendous cost it has upon us physically, emotionally, and spiritually. It is my prayer as a writer that at the end of our journey together you will fully discover what it means to serve with joy. So let the journey begin.

Acknowledgements

No one can be effective in ministry (or in publishing) without the assistance of others. This begins with my wife. She is not just my best friend and closest companion, but she is truly my fellow worker in the ministry. Without her, I would never have survived the challenges of ministry. I am also grateful for my church and the love and support they have shown over the years. While there have been the joys and struggles, their support has been an evidence of God's grace. I would also like to express my appreciation for the counsel I received from Vern Wilkinson and his input into the project. I would be remiss if I did not especially thank John Rainey and Paul Brinkerhoff. John proved to be an excellent proofreader who constantly improved my writing, and Paul provided superb editing skills and invaluable input to make the project complete. Last, special thanks as well for Jim Weaver and his willingness to publish the book. Each of these individuals is not only valuable contributors to the project, but, more importantly, valuable contributors to the cause of Christ.

1

The Weeping Shepherd

FROM PASSION TO PAIN

"Jesus wept."

The brevity of those words in John chapter 11 serves to heighten both the shock and unexpectedness of them. The intrigue only intensifies when we realize that they appear without any grammatical connection to the proceeding verse and without any further explanation. The brevity of the statement causes the reader to stop and ponder: Why did Jesus weep? Was it merely because Lazarus, his close friend, was dead? But why would Jesus weep for Lazarus's death when he already knew the outcome would be Lazarus's resurrection? Was it because he empathized with the grief of Mary and Martha? Was it because of the failure of the people to see beyond the present and see the hope of the resurrection? Was it because of his grief over the deadly effects of sin? Perhaps it goes far deeper than any of these.

The term used in verse 35 of John chapter 11 is a different word than the weeping expressed by Mary. The term used of Jesus' grief refers to a silent, more severe weeping—a grief too deep for words. New Testament scholar A. T. Robertson puts this verse's significance in perspective: "This is the shortest verse in the Bible, but no verse carries more meaning in it."[1] This short verse draws us into the heart

---

[1] Archibald Thomas Robertson, *Word Pictures in the New Testament*, 6 vols. (1930–33; repr., Grand Rapids: Baker, 1980), 5:203.

of a shepherd. To be a shepherd of people is to experience deep and profound grief.

Although couched in slightly different language, two other times we find reference to Jesus weeping. He wept over the rebellion and sinfulness of Jerusalem (Luke 19:41). He wept when confronted with the full weight of the suffering he was to experience upon the cross (Heb. 5:7). However, in these verses we find encapsulated the reality that Jesus was "a man of sorrows and acquainted with grief" (Isa. 53:3).

Being a shepherd involves more than watching over the flock; it involves entering into the realm of distress and grief. A shepherd cannot remain detached and indifferent. A shepherd experiences the pain and sorrow of a broken world set on rejecting the very one who came to deliver them. This brings a high cost both professionally and personally, one that can easily overwhelm us and drive us from ministry. As shepherds, the question is not whether we will experience profound grief. The question we face is whether or not we will be able to maintain our perspective in the midst of the burden and discomfort of ministry. To be a shepherd is to weep!

The Cost of Leaving the Ministry

The news is tragic enough. Another pastor resigned not only from a church, but ministry as well. Having served several different churches with a passion for evangelism and equipping the saints, the pastor finally had enough. Broken, disillusioned with ministry, with the church, and even with God himself, he resigned. But what makes the story so tragic is that it is repeated over and over again. Pastors leave the pulpit broken by the pressures and stresses. Sometimes they leave emotionally drained and burned out. Other times they leave because they failed to give attention to their own emotional and spiritual well-being, becoming easy prey for temptation and sin. Others leave discouraged and frustrated with the daily struggles.

According to one study 40 percent of pastors left the ministry within the first ten years of ministry, and 60 percent left within twenty years.[2] In another study of pastors in the Nazarene denomination, 42 percent of their pastors left the ministry after fifteen years in ministry.[3] While many leave the ministry because of the distress they experienced, those who remain often experience significant trauma by forced resignations. While they move on to serve another church, the strain they experience leaves permanent scars upon their souls. Often when pastors leave a church they do so because of pressure put upon them to resign. One study suggests that only 15 to 25 percent of pastors leave a specific ministry completely voluntarily.[4] However, the statistics, as disturbing as they are, do not tell the whole story. For when a pastor leaves a church because of pressures and stress, it not only exacts an enormous emotional toll upon the church, upon the pastor, and upon the pastor's family, but it also results in a spiritual crisis.

What I'm saying here applies in principle just as much to those who have served as elders, deacons and deaconesses, or whoever may be discouraged in their ministry, whether a pastor or a Sunday school teacher. While my background and experience focuses on the pastor as the lead minister of a local church, what I am saying about suffering in the course of doing ministry is for all who serve the Lord and his people whatever terminology is used or denominational tradition gives structure to the daily tasks, duties, and expectations of a shepherd. The message and perspective offered is for anyone who has engaged in ministry and consequently experienced suffering in the line of duty.

When I started ministry together with my wife and best friend, Becky, by my side, we had a clear sense of God's calling upon our lives.

---

[2] Dean R. Hoge and Jacqueline E. Wegner, *Pastors in Transition: Why Clergy Leave Local Church Ministry* (Grand Rapids: Eerdmans, 2005). 28.

[3] Charles Stone, *Five Ministry Killers and How to Defeat Them: Help for Frustrated Pastors—Including New Research from the Barna Group* (Minneapolis: Bethany, 2010), 43.

[4] Hoge and Wenger, *Pastors in Transition*, 45.

We believed God ordained us to this task. We shared the same feeling Paul expressed in the letter to the church at Corinth when he wrote, "For if I preach the gospel, I have nothing to boast of, for I am under compulsion; for woe is me if I do not preach the gospel" (1 Cor. 9:16) There inwardly burned a compulsion of the Spirit to serve Christ faithfully and be a part of his eternal work of building the church. Countless pastors and preachers throughout church history shared and experienced this same passion. In a sense this distinguishes the ministry from any other occupation. It is not just that we enjoy the ministry and feel called to it, but that we can do nothing else.

Tragically, as time moves forward, the inner passion becomes an inward pain. The "fire in the belly" begins to smolder and is eventually extinguished by the pressures, discouragements, and rejections we feel. This leads to the inward turmoil of the soul. Our experience does not match our expectations. Consequently, we begin to wonder if God somehow mistakenly chose us, or if we misinterpreted the call of God. When the latter happens, we begin to doubt our ability to know God's will. If we were mistaken about this, how can we be certain of anything that we might believe about God's direction for our life? But worse is when the former happens—God must have made a mistake. This leads to a crisis of faith. How can God be good when he appointed us to a task that he failed to equip us to perform? Fellow shepherd Kent Hughes captures this conflict of faith when he writes of the inward struggle he faced in his ministry, including debates about it with his wife, Barbara.

I went on, "In cold statistics my chances of being a failure are overwhelming. Most pastors do little more than survive in the ministry in piddly little churches." I rehearsed how a professor had stood before my seminary class and said that eight out of ten will never pastor a church larger than 150 people. These were the statistics. And if true, they condemned most pastors to subsistence living unless their wives worked outside the home. "The ministry is asking too much of me," I said to Barbara. "How can I go on giving all that I have without seeing results, especially when others are?" I had been working day and night with no visible return. Everyone needs to see results. Farmers see their crops grow. It is their proper reward. I could see others' "crops" grow, but my field bore nothing. . . .

"Those who really make it in the ministry are those with exceptional gifts. If I had a great personality or natural charisma, if I had celebrity status, a deep resonant voice, a merciless executive ability, a domineering personality that doesn't mind sacrificing people for success, I could make it to the top. Where is God in all of this?" I defied Barbara to disprove me. "Just look at the great preachers today. Their success seems to have little to do with God's Spirit; they're just superior people!"

Suddenly I found myself coming to the conclusion that I didn't want to admit. Though I knew it had been brooding in me for quite some time, now it was finally coming out. "God has called me to do something he hasn't given me the gifts to accomplish. Therefore, God is not good."[5]

These sentiments echo the words of C. S. Lewis when he summarizes for his readers the problem of pain in its simplest form: "If God were good, He would wish to make His creatures perfectly happy, and if God were almighty He would be able to do what He wished. But the creatures are not happy. Therefore God lacks either goodness, or power, or both."[6] We struggle with the same question when we confront the trials of ministry. If God is good and powerful, why do we continue to flounder, striving to obtain his blessing, but never seeming to experience it?

The Cost to Our Faith in God

When we contemplate leaving the ministry to pursue a different vocation, we experience further inward turmoil. Leaving results in a crisis of faith as we struggle with a sense of guilt and failure that goes to our

---

[5]   Kent and Barbara Hughes, *Liberating Ministry from the Success Syndrome* (Wheaton, IL: Tyndale, 1987), 22–23.

[6]   C. S. Lewis, *The Problem of Pain* (1940; repr., New York: Macmillan, 1978), 26.

very soul. What started out as a call from God ends in the ash heap of spiritual despair. When a pastor leaves a church, it does more than just bring a loss of livelihood and upheaval for the family. It leads to an intense inward conflict of the spirit. To abandon ministry brings about a crisis of our faith and what we believe about God.[7]

We sense the spiritual compulsion Paul expressed when he saw his appointment to the apostleship occurring even before he was born (Gal. 1:15). So compelling is this call, he could do nothing else. He must preach, not just because it was his desire, but because he was under a divine obligation. Not to preach was to face dire punishment from God.

When we stand before the congregation each week, we fully realize that we cannot perform the ministry based upon our innate qualities and abilities but only by divine empowerment. The anticipation of God's empowerment leads us to the crisis within our struggles. If God empowered us with his supernatural strength, then how can we falter? Why do we live in the realm of failure rather than success? But quitting is not an option. We begin to question everything we believe about God.

The question "Why do you not believe in God?" faces not only atheists but also battle-weary and beleaguered shepherds who like the man in the Gospel say to Jesus, "I do believe; help my unbelief" (Mark 9:24). C. S. Lewis points to this crisis of pain when he argues as he did when he was an atheist that the pain in the world serves as evidence that God does not exist: "If you ask me to believe that this [the pain and destruction in the universe] is the work of a benevolent and omnipotent spirit, I reply that all the evidence points in the opposite direction. Either there is no spirit behind the universe, or else a spirit indifferent to good and evil, or else an evil spirit."[8] This is often the very paradox

---

[7]   I am indebted to Kent and Barbara Hughes for providing insight and understanding of the impact that the struggles in ministry have upon our attitude towards God, the church, and ourselves. Hughes and Hughes, *Liberating Ministry from the Success Syndrome*, 22–23.

[8]   Lewis, *Problem of Pain*, 15.

with which we struggle. If God is good, how could he allow us to face so many trials when we serve him? Yet for Lewis, he came to realize that the very reality of pain became the testimony of both God's existence and his goodness.

Lewis goes on to point out, "If the universe is so bad, or even half so bad, how on earth did human beings ever come to attribute it to the activity of a wise and good Creator? Men are fools, perhaps; but hardly so foolish as that. The direct inference from black to white, from evil flower to virtuous root, from senseless work to a workman infinitely wise, staggers belief. The spectacle of the universe as revealed by experience can never have been the ground of religion: it must always have been something in spite of which religion, acquired from a different source, was held."[9] That source could only have been God. Rather than the reality of pain destroying our faith, it serves to buttress it. The very thing that would seem to deny the existence of God affirms it. Pain does not point us to a God who causes it or remains indifferent to it. Pain points us to a world that is indelibly broken, a world only God can fix.

The Cost to Our View of the Church

Leaving the ministry results in a crisis in our view of the church. Even if we do not feel abandoned by God, we feel abandoned by the church. When we enter ministry we do so with a vision of impacting the world and leading people who are hungry to know God and live in obedience to him. However, we soon find that the church is not as receptive to our preaching as we thought. If we preach against sin, we are judgmental; if we preach on love, then we cater to the crowds. If we preach exegetical messages, we are too academic; if we preach topically, then all we are preaching is biblical fluff. If we maintain the status quo, we lack vision; if we try to implement change, we are insensitive and dictatorial. The list could go on. People continually place unrealistic and conflicting expectations upon us.

---

[9] Ibid., 15.

When we leave the church, we often feel used by the church. We often feel that people treated us as chattel, sucking us spiritually and emotionally dry and then disregarding us when we cry out for help. Furthermore, we feel abandoned by the denomination that promised so much support. This is especially true for the small church pastors who, even in the best of times, feel forgotten and looked down upon by denominational leaders. Instead of providing support in our time of need, they continue to pursue their own agenda, too busy to address the problems we face. Consequently, we become disillusioned both with the church and with the denominational leaders.

The Cost to Our View of Ourselves

Finally, leaving the ministry results in a crisis in our view of ourselves. Ministry can elevate the ego or destroy it. It can lead to pride or it can lead to self-abasement. If things are going well and people sing our praise, we can start to believe that we are special. But when things start to go badly, it can undermine our assessment of our position in Christ. We affirm in our understanding of justification that God sees us as positionally righteous, even in spite of our daily failures. But we often forget the sanctifying process that must take place. Positionally we are declared righteous, but we have yet to attain what God has already ordained, so we still struggle with sin and its grip upon our life. Thus, when problems arise in ministry, we attribute it to our personal failures and in so doing nullify both our justification as well as the sanctifying work of the Holy Spirit. We forget that God is more concerned about what he is doing *in* us than what he is doing *through* us. In order for God to bring about the growth in us he will often take us through painful experiences to mold and shape us into Christ's image. Consequently, when we leave the ministry we experience a sense of disillusionment with ourselves. Not only do we begin to doubt our abilities, but also we begin to doubt the validity of our relationship with God.

THE UNRELENTING SEARCH FOR ANSWERS

Even for those who remain steadfast in the ministry, there remains an inward battle. While we continue to toil, we inwardly envy those who left. We wonder what life would be like without the constant face of failure and brokenness staring at us. We strive to faithfully preach the Word and pursue after the will and purpose of God for our families, our churches, and ourselves yet wonder if we somehow missed the road signs of God's plan.

What is the cause of this crisis? Is it the church and their failure to support the pastor and recognize his humanness? Is it God and his failure to give us the emotional and spiritual wisdom to deal with all the problems we face? Is it our own inabilities? Or is it a failure to understand the very nature of ministry itself and what it is that God has actually called us to be and do? These questions plague us in the midst of our struggles. They haunt us like a specter at night when we cannot sleep, causing not only doubt in terms of our ministry, but also in our understanding of God. For the psalmist, resting securely in God enables a person to lie down and sleep (Ps. 4:8). Yet when these questions haunt the nights, not only do we find sleep fleeting, but we even begin to wonder if God has fallen asleep and so he is not taking notice of our plight (Ps. 44:23–26). Instead of finding answers, we often face the unrelenting onslaught of questions.

In reality there are no easy, simplistic answers. Many of the circumstances that cause our pain and result in this crisis remain outside our control. While there are many helpful books that deal with principles to help a person alleviate and cope with the stress and struggle confronting us, the reality remains that we still live with inward fears.[10] While we

---

[10] For some helpful books that deal with managing the stress and emotional turmoil of ministry, see Anne Jackson, *Mad Church Disease: Overcoming the Burnout Epidemic* (Grand Rapids: Zondervan, 2009); G. Lloyd Rediger, *Clergy Killers: Guidance for Pastors and Congregations Under Attack* (1996; Louisville: Westminster John Knox Press,

cannot change our circumstances, nor can we avoid or resolve all the problems, we can change our response. But to do this, we must do more than change our reactions, we must change our perspective.

In order to think rightly about the challenges confronting us, it is necessary that we go back to the pages of Scripture. In 2 Peter 1:3 God promises that "His divine power has granted to us everything pertaining to life and godliness, through the true knowledge of Him who called us by his own glory and excellence." This divine enablement comes through our knowledge of Christ that is grounded in Scripture. Scripture drives and determines our theology, and our theology undergirds and forms our perspective. The more we know God, his being and his activity, and our required response, the more equipped we are to live the life he called us to live and manifest the godliness he desires to instill within us.

Our theology is more than just a set of statements meant to summarize in creedal form what we intellectually assent to. Theology governs and determines our worldview. It serves to define the lens through which we view all of life and all the events that occur. It provides the basis for how we understand, interpret, and respond to every situation and circumstance. Theology is what we believe about who God is, what he does, and how we (and all creation) respond to him. Consequently, our theology ultimately defines and dictates our relationship with God and the way we live our faith in everyday circumstances. What we believe is not just an academic statement. It is how we live. We do not merely glean our theology from a set of creedal statements formulated by the church. We develop our theology from the self-revelation of God communicated in the pages of Scripture. The knowledge of God begins with the knowledge of his Word (Ps.

1997); Charles Stone, *Five Ministry Killers and How to Defeat Them: Help for Frustrated Pastors—Including New Research from the Barna Group* (Minneapolis: Bethany, 2010); Wayne Cordeiro, *Leading on Empty: Refilling Your Tank and Renewing Your Passion* (Minneapolis: Bethany, 2009); and Eric O. Rogers, *Wounded Minister: Reflections of a Former Pastor* (New York: iUniverse, 2006).

19:7–14). As the Scriptures inform and mold our understanding of God, it alters our view of the world in which we live. Conversely, how we understand the world gives a window into our soul, revealing the real theology governing our life.

Tragically, there is often a disconnect between the theology we claim and the theology by which we live. While we affirm a traditional understanding of God, often we are more influenced by contemporary and cultural "theology" that is often contrary to the professions we make. For example, we believe in the sufficiency of Scripture yet feel as if we need more than just the Bible to be effective in ministry. We affirm that the Holy Spirit empowers us for service but continually question our ability to perform the task to which God has called us. We acknowledge that we will face persecution because of our faith yet feel cheated when we encounter suffering. When our theology and perspective becomes skewed, our response to circumstances becomes flawed.

While most books focus on our emotional response to the stress that paralyzes us, the purpose of this book is to reexamine our understanding of ministry. While we often cannot change our circumstances, we can change our point of view. When approaching the issue of suffering, two approaches can be taken. The first approach focuses upon the emotional impact of trials. This approach deals with the emotions that arise when we go through painful circumstances. There are a number of books that spotlight this aspect of suffering. This does not discount the validity and value such books bring in helping us overcome the trauma of ministry. They are beneficial and helpful. This book is not meant to address the emotional burnout that comes through the relentless pursuit of ministry. While I hope that this book will touch the readers emotions and bring healing to the emotional and spiritual scars that ministry brings, my greatest hope is that it will thoroughly change how we think, for it is the renewing of the mind that generates genuine and lasting change (Rom. 12:2). While it is important to deal with emotional scars from ministry (and others more qualified than I speak to these issues), it is equally important that we change our perspective on how we understand and process the circumstances we face in life.

The second approach, and the intent of this book, is to look at suffering from a theological perspective. The goal of this study is to examine the biblical teaching regarding suffering in order that we might regain a proper perspective in the midst of the struggles we face. Not only does suffering often create an emotional crisis leading to depression, burnout, and feelings of despair, it creates a theological crisis as well. In this book we shall take a journey through Scripture, a journey that seeks to address the question "What is the biblical perspective on suffering and ministry?" While this book may not answer all the questions that we have when we face trials, it is prayerfully hoped that it will serve as a starting point.

We will never be free from the problems and challenges that come with the calling and work of shepherding God's flock, but we can view our suffering differently, even as Paul did when he stated that he had learned the secret of being content in all circumstances both good and bad (Phil. 4:11–13). Nevertheless, the secret is not easily learned. We do not learn to be content by sitting in an armchair gazing at our navels. It requires a journey, a walk on a path that just might take us to the dark side of suffering.

2

Pain and Ministry

UNDERSTANDING THE COST

Sometimes we wonder if God is a merciless prankster. Recall when you entered ministry. You desired to make a difference, right? No one desires to be a failure, to flounder and end up on the back burner of ministry where little seems to get accomplished for the name of Christ. We read the pages of Acts and stand amazed at the profound influence of the early church. We study church history and read of the individuals who made a difference not only in their local setting but on the universal church as well. As we read about their lives, we take further hope in the fact that many of these individuals were not supersaints. They were normal individuals who struggled with the same failures and shortcomings that we ourselves experience. Yet, for all their faults and personal warts, God used them to build his kingdom and grow the church. Likewise, God can use us and so we begin ministry with the same desires and expectations.

But reality often does not match expectations. Instead of experiencing success and growth, many shepherds soon confront the continual struggle just to maintain the existing attendance in the church. We begin to wonder, "What happened to the blessing of God upon our ministry?" It is not without reason that a primary struggle pastors face is a sense of futility. When we go home at the end of the day, we often wonder if we have accomplished anything for the kingdom. Instead of seeing lives changed, we question whether or not our messages are falling on deaf ears. When confronted with the lack of spiritual growth, we feel like a mason using a rubber mallet and a plastic chisel trying to crack a heart of stone. The call of God seems more like a cruel joke than a sacred and privileged calling. Instead of sensing God's loving involvement in our ministry, we are tempted to question if God gleefully laughs at our gullibility in believing that somehow he would actually use the likes of us to alter the eternal destinies of people within the church and community.

Depressing indeed, isn't it? It is no wonder that many Monday mornings we find ourselves defeated, ready to send in our resignation. The one day when everyone should most rejoice that God has once again faithfully communicated his eternal Word with its life-transforming power, we feel empty and beaten down, ready to throw in the proverbial towel. Am I exaggerating? You'll know I'm not if you've been there.

So how do we reconcile our experiences and frustrations with the anticipated joy of ministry? Our initial and normal reaction is to question our calling. We begin to wonder if we chose the wrong profession. At other times, we question our training and education. We face problems and issues feeling too ill-equipped to handle them and so we fault the seminary, blaming them for our shortcomings. But even as we criticize our training, we sense an inward awareness that the issues go far beyond any perceived fault of our professors.

In the quietness of our inward soul, we are painfully aware of our own sinfulness, and so we begin to wonder if our own failures and inward spiritual shortcomings prevent God from pouring out his blessings upon our life. While our theology confesses that we are saved by grace and justified fully by the gracious act of Christ upon the cross, inwardly we believe that somehow we must earn God's blessing. We reason that if we lived righteous enough, God would bless our church. Conversely, when things go the proverbial south, we attribute it to our own inability to earn God's blessing.

What Brian Hedges writes about Christians in general is equally true for pastors and others serving the Lord and his people:

All too often, religious people view their acts of piety or moral efforts as a means of gaining acceptance with God. Check yourself now. Even if you've been a Christian for a long time, don't you sometimes feel like God is more pleased with you on days when you've been faithful in daily devotions than those rushed days when you neglect time in the Word and prayer? . . .

. . . [O]ur relationship with God can easily become based on our own performance, rather than the performance of Christ. Even good spiritual disciplines, such as Bible-reading, prayer, and worship, become in our minds, like rungs on the ladder to heave. We may not express it this way. In fact, we might even deny it. But functionally, and practically, we live as if approval from God depended upon our obedience, instead of Christ's obedience for us."[1]

This can often be said of us. If we remain faithful in devotions and prayer, then we feel that we will be under God's blessing, and if things start going badly, we blame it on the shortfalls in our personal pursuit of sanctification. Consequently, we become driven by guilt and fear.

Early in ministry, I remember the statement an older minister made: "As a pastor we always live with guilt—guilt that we have not worked hard enough, been spiritual enough, or done enough in ministry." Having now been in the pastorate for almost thirty years, I can fully identify with the truthfulness of his statement. Nothing would please us more than to hear God say those often-quoted words, "Well done, thou good and faithful servant" (Matt. 25:21 KJV). Yet we often wonder if this remains the pursuit of the unattainable.

However, we face not only the challenge to define justification as it relates to God's blessing, but also the appearance of the apparent success of churches and pastors who are not serving with right motives or even a biblical theology. Instead of seeking to build the kingdom of Christ, it seems as if they are more focused upon building their own kingdom. How can God bless their ministry with misguided priorities and motivations and yet not bless our own when we are striving to do what pleases God? Are we struggling in vain? If God blesses a

---

[1] Brian Hedges, *Christ Formed in You: The Power of the Gospel for Personal Change* (Wapwallopen, PA: Shepherd Press, 2010), 71–72.

ministry based upon our merit, do we possess any hope for our ministry? If God's blessing is not based on any acts of righteousness, then why should we struggle so much to live righteously? Here again we overlook the sanctifying work of Christ in our life and that it is often through the trials, rather than the triumphs, that God achieves the greatest amount of spiritual growth.

Understanding and working in the context of the anguish and turmoil of ministry becomes further compounded by our cultural point of view. In our North American culture, we are widely influenced by the idea that happiness and prosperity indicate God's blessing. We see pleasure and happiness as the ultimate right of each individual. While in our theological worldview we reject the health and wealth, "name it, claim it" theology, we nevertheless have been influenced by it through the cultural lens that governs our outlook. Even within the most ardent opponent of prosperity theology, there is the hidden perception that stubbornly ties prosperity (and even church growth and ministry success) with God's blessing. We often unconsciously reason that if we are under the blessing of God, then our churches will be growing. We define a successful ministry by numerical growth. Consequently, when we do experience problems and frustrations we feel like God has withdrawn his blessing. We may have been called by God, but, like Job, at times we wonder if God has abandoned us.

Ministry and Suffering

The stark reality is that the call to ministry is a call to suffering. Candid conversations with pastors reveal a variety of challenges, problems, frustrations, and difficulties. Some of our struggles are extremely intense while others are more of a dull pain. Some crash upon us like a wave only to quickly recede while others rise up like a tsunami with a wave the just keeps coming and rising until it swallows us up. None of us can ever forget the videos of the tsunami that struck Japan. It was not the monster wall of water, towering above everything that we often see in movies. Rather, it was a relentless surge that just kept rising until it finally engulfed everything in its path. So it is in ministry. The momentary wave of trouble that comes quickly and recedes we can survive, but the steady onslaught that seems to have no end eventually beats us down until we feel like we are drowning.

In this we are not alone, for the apostle Paul speaks candidly about his own difficulties. At times he rejoiced in his suffering as he saw it as part of his identification with Christ and with his suffering. In Colossians 1:24 he writes, "Now I rejoice in my sufferings for your sake, and in my flesh I do my share on behalf of His body, which is the church, in filling up what is lacking in Christ's afflictions." For Paul, the persecution and opposition he experienced was not just directed at him, but was part of the suffering of Christ. He saw his affliction not just as a part of the Christian life, but a part of his relationship with Christ. Furthermore, he did not see the anguish he experienced as arbitrary and without rhyme or reason. Rather, it was necessary if he was to build up the church. This perspective of suffering stemmed from the very call of Paul. When Christ miraculously redeemed Paul from the clutches of his legalistic world, Christ made it clear through Ananias that "he must suffer for My name's sake" (Acts 9:16). The calling of God that Paul so desperately sought to fulfill was calling to cease persecuting Christians and instead to identify with them, a calling that would cost him dearly at all levels of his life.

However, Paul did not always have such a positive attitude regarding his suffering, for there were other times when he revealed the deep pain and distress he experienced. He captures the physical, emotional, mental, and spiritual turmoil he experienced in 2 Corinthians 11:23–29:

> Are they servants of Christ?—I speak as if insane—I more so; in far more labors, in far more imprisonments, beaten times without number, often in danger of death. Five times I received from the Jews thirty-nine lashes. Three times I was beaten with rods, once I was stoned, three times I was shipwrecked, a night and a day I have spent in the deep. I have been on frequent journeys, in dangers from rivers, dangers from

robbers, dangers from my countrymen, dangers from the Gentiles, dangers in the city, dangers in the wilderness, dangers on the sea, dangers among false brethren; I have been in labor and hardship, through many sleepless nights, in hunger and thirst, often without food, in cold and exposure. Apart from such external things, there is the daily pressure on me of concern for all the churches. Who is weak without my being weak? Who is led into sin without my intense concern?

For those who sought to lead the church in the first century, ministry did not bring financial security and personal blessing. Rather, it brought the person into the arena of personal pain, not just because of direct physical persecution, but inwardly from the pressures and challenges of moving people from where they want to be (comfortable pew sitters) to where they do not want to be (in the battlefront of spiritual ministry) and to give up what they want to possess (their personal self-interests) so that they might possess what they do not desire (the character of Christ that brings self-sacrifice). All the while, we face the inward struggles of our own personal shortcomings and our own propensity to "wander from the God we love." Paul pointed to these inward battles when refers to his own inward fears: "For even when we came into Macedonia our flesh had no rest, but we were afflicted on every side: conflicts without, *fears within*" (2 Cor. 7:5).

WHEN THE SPARKS FLY UPWARD

In their misguided and frequently hurtful attempt to counsel Job, his three friends reveal a distorted understanding not only of Job and his character, but also of the very nature of suffering (we will talk further about this in chapter 4). For them travails were a part of the sinful world that could only be resolved by personal repentance. At the start of their haranguing Job, Eliphaz makes the statement that "man is born to trouble as surely as sparks fly upward" (Job 5:7 NIV). At times, this picture resonates with our own problems. People enjoy sitting around a campfire and watching the dancing glow of the fire and feeling its warmth. As the darkness descends, the air is soon filled with glowing embers that flee upward in the updraft of the flames. You don't need to be a physics major to recognize the validity of Elipaz's statement regarding the dancing of the flames. When you touch the logs upon the fire to reposition of them, the air is suddenly filled with sparks that escape the final clutches of the flames. As we are entrenched in the daily affairs of ministry, we cannot help but be troubled by the comparison. Just as it is inevitable that flames send a cascade of sparks upward, so we will face the certainty of our own troubles.

However, the difficulty in any discussion of suffering is that what may be overwhelmingly painful and debilitating to one seems minor to another. Consequently, any discussion on the various causes of discouragement must be done with the awareness that examples are not meant to be typical of each person. Rather, they are representative of the type of issues that we might be struggling with. Furthermore, just because the majority of other pastors do not suffer in a particular area does not minimize the intensity of suffering experienced by the ones who do. For example, one pastor may be untouched and unconcerned by unjust criticism while another becomes paralyzed by it.

We must recognize that we are unique individuals who respond to circumstances, situations, and pressures differently. While we may not all respond the same to a particular issue, each of us will face significant problems that cause us to become discouraged and question our call and qualifications. Furthermore, the inward anxiety grows more intense because we serve in areas where we become isolated from others. We are isolated from denominational support. We lack the contact with other pastors or mentors who can empathize with our hurt. Because we are the pastor, our position even isolates us from people within our own church. Whether we identify with the seven issues mentioned in what follows below or not, we are painfully aware that we do face a number of troubles in each of our own particular ministries that seem to overwhelm us at times and cause us to wonder if maybe another profession would be a better choice.

The Pain of Discouragement and Futility

Having served the same church for over twenty years, sometimes I wonder if my time has accomplished anything. The same people seem to struggle with the same temptations that they were dealing with twenty years ago. While a few seem to catch fire and grow exponentially, the rest seem to remain cemented in the same struggles, problems, and sins year after year. It is no wonder then that 80 percent of pastors and 84 percent of their spouses are discouraged or dealing with depression.[2] For many pastors, the greatest frustration they face is the feelings of futility.

The reason we become discouraged is because we do not see immediate results for our labors, and many times we fail to see any results at all. We continually labor without any sense of accomplishment and achievement. Consequently, we begin to question not just our call, but the power and validity of the gospel itself. When Christ states that he will build his church and the gates of Hades will not prevail against it, we inwardly laugh thinking that "Christ never knew about our church." Added to our feelings of futility are the reports that even those in the pew do not believe we have any significant influence. In a survey conducted, only 37 percent of Americans believe that the clergy make a big contribution to society. Even among those who attend church regularly, the figure remains at only 52 percent.[3] Barna Group's research found that Americans feel that professional athletes have more influence than pastors.[4] In a culture where people are more obsessed by the latest ex-

---

[2] Charles Stone, *Five Ministry Killers and How to Defeat Them: Help for Frustrated Pastors—Including New Research from the Barna Group* (Minneapolis: Bethany, 2010), 33.

[3] "Public Esteem for the Military Still High," Pew Research Center Religion and Public Life Project, July 11, 2013, accessed July 23, 2013, http://www.pewforum.org/Other-Demographics/Public-Esteem-for-Military-Still-High.aspx#middling.

[4] Jeremy Weber, "Pro Athletes Influence Society More Than Pastors, Say Two-Thirds of Americans," *Christianity Today*, posted February 1, 2013, accessed July 23, 2013, http://www.christianitytoday.com/gleanings/2013/february/pro-athletes-influence-society-more-than-pastors-say-two.html.

ploits of the famous than they are about the moral guidelines of Scripture, where they spend more time reading the *National Enquirer* than they do the Bible, it is hard to remain relevant in the eyes of people. It is no wonder that we often question if we have any impact at all.

But we do not stand alone in this, for even Elijah wrestled with the same question because of his experience on Mount Carmel. After his resounding and miraculous victory over the prophets of Baal, Elijah expected a mass revival in which the nation of Israel would collectively turn back to the monotheistic worship of Yahweh. However, after his powerful demonstration the people responded with a collective yawn as they remained in their polytheistic idolatry, and Jezebel was hellbent on taking Elijah's life. Elijah had enough. When he fled into the desert, he was not seeking to hide from Jezebel. Instead, utterly dejected and discouraged, he concluded that there was no longer any hope for Israel and that the covenant was irreparably broken.

Like each one of us when we leave seminary or a similar place of training to enter ministry, Elijah had a vision of God doing incredible things through him, only to see those dreams dashed on the rocks of an apathetic people with hearts of stone. So, like the prophet Elijah, when confronted with the lack of any great successes, we conclude that we are no better than all the other pastors who left ministry disillusioned, discouraged, and in despair.

Paul faced the same tension when he wrote to the church in Corinth. The church should have matured beyond the petty arguments and conflicts that plagued them. However, Paul had to go back to the very foundation of the gospel to remind them that the gospel was not about people, but about the person of Christ: "And I, brethren, could not speak to you as to spiritual men, but as to men of flesh, as to infants in Christ. I gave you milk to drink, not solid food; for you were not yet able to receive it. Indeed, even now you are not yet able, for you are still fleshly. For since there is jealousy and strife among you, are you not fleshly, and are you not walking like mere men?" (1 Cor. 3:1–3).

The plague of discouragement strikes when we often fail to see dramatic results. Evangelistic programs that seemed to work so well in other communities fail to achieve even one convert in our own community. We develop programs to equip, train, and challenge people to become involved in the ministry of the church only to see them make one excuse after another about why they cannot be involved. Small groups seem to flounder because of people's failure to place it as a priority. The Sunday school continues its slow descent even though we have passionate teachers who deeply care about the kids. So we doggedly continue, always seeking to find the key that would unlock the hearts of people, but never seeming to find it.

As we continue to march faithfully along, we wonder what happened to the power of the gospel of grace that Paul so passionately defended. We become lost in the search for the transformational message. We rightly recognize that if we claim credit for our success then we undermine grace. In attributing our success to our abilities we nullify grace. Yet, we wonder if the lack of success stems from our own failure. But in the end, this too undermines grace. When we attribute the lack of growth in the church to our personal failures and shortcomings, we equally deny God's grace. In so doing we deny that his grace governs all aspects of our life. The end result is that works become the basis for blessing and grace becomes absent.

The Pain of Numbers and Personal Validation

As pastors we always dream of the day when our church would overflow. Not that we expect or even want to become a megachurch, but that we would see some level of numerical growth that would validate our ministry. Lest than 0.5 percent of churches today average over 2,000, and 60 percent of all churches have fewer than 100 people in attendance. Even though the megachurch, and even the large church (more than 500), is the anomaly, we are continually told that they provide the benchmark of success.[5] We have become convinced that the numerical growth and

---

[5]   Hartford Institute for Religious Research, "Fast Facts about American Religion" accessed March 3, 2015, http://hirr.hartsem.edu/research/fastfacts/fast_facts.html.

size of the church provides the final confirmation of our ministry. Yet the reality is that many churches across America face a steady decline. As society has become more secular both morally and religiously, people no longer see the necessity for church. Furthermore, we are told that an estimated 75 percent of young people who were raised in the church no longer attend. If the trend continues, humanly speaking we wonder if there will be a church in the future. Even though these statistics have been challenged by some and other data suggest that things are not as dire as they first appear, it does not placate us.[6] We have already been convinced that evangelicalism stands on the precipice of collapse.

If these figures are not discouraging enough, the latest books continually tell us that the problem lies with us, and that we as pastors are failing to adequately do our job. Pastor and author Charles Stone writes, "Disappointment with pastors tops disappointment with other church relationships as a main reason people leave."[7] The implication is that we are failing, that if we would communicate better, judge less, preach more relevant messages, and so forth, then we would be growing. While we recognize theologically that numbers do not provide the most reliable indicators of success, in reality we remain convinced that numbers affirm our self-worth and validate our ministry.

When our validation shifts from the proclamation of truth to outward, visible results measured by growth, it distorts our role in ministry. When people evaluate us by the number of people in the pews, they begin to develop unrealistic expectations of pastors. Instead of being communicators of truth who challenge people to holiness, we become pop psychologists whose purpose is to make people happy rather than holy. Our task becomes both undefined and unattainable. Like a woman who always compares herself to a supermodel, so we are measured

---

[6] There are studies that would indicate that the perceived decline in the American Church is not as dramatic as some would have us to believe. See Bradley R. E. Wright, *Christians Are Hate-Filled Hypocrites . . . and Other Lies You've Been Told* (Minneapolis: Bethany, 2010).

[7] Stone, *Five Ministry Killers and How to Defeat Them*, 36.

by how well we stack up to the pastors who populate the airwaves. But, in reality, both are a false illusion. Just as the supermodel is a product of airbrushing, Photoshop, surgery, and unhealthy dieting, so the people's view of the superpastor becomes a false illusion. Pastors on the radio, television, and Internet are in reality creations of our own mind. We make them and their message into what we want them to be. We create virtual pastors who conform to our desires (after all if I do not like the message, I change the channel) instead of having a pastor who confronts us in person with the need for a radical change in our identity.

Because people have created a false illusion of what a pastor is to be, they become critical of any pastor who falls short. In this, the pastor of the small church becomes especially vulnerable. The size of the large church enables people to maintain their idealistic illusion because they never get to know the weaknesses of the real person behind the pulpit. But this is not true of the small church. There, everyone knows the pastor on an individual level, and so it does not take long for the illusion to turn into disillusionment as they see the pastor with all his shortcomings. This results in criticism and abandonment of the church in search of a pastor who would measure up to the false ideal. This constant criticism leveled at pastors in particular and church leaders in general fails to line up with the biblical perspective of both the church and the calling to be a pastor.

First, it fails to recognize that pastors, elders, and other teachers in the church are likewise fallen individuals who struggle with sin, failings, and inadequacies. Ultimately, no one is adequate for the task, for we are all incompetent. As Paul points out in 2 Corinthians 3:5–6, "Not that we are adequate in ourselves to consider anything as coming from ourselves, but our adequacy is from God, who also made us adequate as servants of a new covenant, not of the letter but of the Spirit; for the letter kills, but the Spirit gives life." When people expect only perfection in the pastor, it is not the fault of the pastor; rather it is the fault of the people who are denying the reality of grace operating in the life of the pastor.

Second, criticism fails to recognize that the pastor is ultimately not the one responsible for the growth of the church. Paul is clear—the growth of the church is the responsibility of the sovereign God who works in the hearts and minds of people. He put it plainly to the Corinthians: "So then neither the one who plants nor the one who waters is anything, but God who causes the growth" (1 Cor. 3:7). To follow specific men (and by implication to reject others) is a mark of the flesh rather than the Spirit (v. 3, quoted earlier).

Last, being susceptible to criticism fails to recognize that as we approach the end of the age, there will be a great falling away where the hardness of the people's heart become more evident (Matt. 24:10–12; 2 Thess. 2:3). While we must continue to proclaim the gospel, we must also recognize that the decrease in attendance may not be a result of the incompetence of the pastor or the church, but a hardening of the heart of a nation that has known the truth but rejected it. God both softens the hearts of people through the proclamation of the gospel as well as hardens their hearts as part of the beginning steps of his impending judgment.

All this undermines the basis by which we validate our personal ministry. Because we validate the authenticity of our ministry by our accomplishments, we set ourselves up for failure. We want the validation of people's admiration of our achievements, but all we see is the unresponsiveness of the world. Like the prophet Isaiah, we anticipate positive results. Isaiah first responded to the call of God with enthusiasm crying out, "Here am I. Send me!" (6:8). But when God warned him that people would respond with indifference, his enthusiasm melted into despair when he cried out, "Lord, how long?" (v. 11). Like us, Isaiah expected his ministry to achieve great revival. But God reminded him that the purpose of ministry is not always to achieve great results, but to achieve God's purpose in the proclamation of truth. That purpose may be realized in the revival of people (as in the case of Jonah), or it may be found in the affirmation of the righteousness of God's judgment upon a rebellious people (as was the case in Ezekiel 2:3–5).

The Pain of Conflict and Inward Anxiety

Conflict plagues the church and destroys people and destroys ministry. It is little wonder that when Paul writes of conflict within the church he warns, "If any man destroys the temple of God, God will destroy him, for the temple of God is holy, and that is what you are" (1 Cor. 3:17). This warning comes in the context of division within the church. God takes seriously tensions that divide and destroy unity within the church. Nevertheless, discord still remains one of the major causes of stress for pastors.

Conflict is especially personal and painful for those who lead the church. When problems arise between two individuals within the church, tension arises within the whole congregation as everyone feels the pressure to either take sides or remain neutral within the conflict. People become unwittingly third parties, not because they want to get involved, but because of the close relationships they have with each of the parties. As their pastor or elder, you get caught in the middle. If you have a personal relationship with the people involved, each of the combatants anticipates that you will naturally side with them. When you attempt to remain neutral, the people involved feel betrayed because you did not side with them. After all, if you are truly their friend, you would naturally support their position. As a result, they then turn on you and you find yourself the object of their anger. Proverbs warns, "Like one who takes a dog by the ears is he who passes by and meddles with strife not belonging to him" (Prov. 26:17). In other words, when you enter into a conflict that is not yours, you will often be the one who gets bit. However, even when we do not enter the conflict, we still feel the pangs of the dog's gnarling teeth. No matter what we do, people turn against us. We face a no-win situation.

Because church leaders become the object of personal attacks, despite their best efforts to remain neutral, they experience an elevated foreboding of anxiety. Because of the wounds they received in church conflicts, they often demonstrate the anxiety and fear of someone suffering from post-traumatic stress disorder (PTSD). Have you experienced this? Whenever the phone rings and someone asks to meet with you, your anxiety levels increase dramatically. You re-experience the trauma of previous events, further increasing apprehension and emotional stress. You experience the physical reactions characteristic of PTSD: pounding heart, muscle tension, sweating, difficulty falling asleep, irritability, and difficulty concentrating. We find ourselves wondering if our job may be at stake. We live and serve in a spiritual battle, and we often face the emotional scars that such a battle brings.

The Pain of Rejection and Loneliness

Ministry is a lonely business. Even though we spend the bulk of our time with others, it is still a lonely task, as a certain lone minister Joel P. Sturtevant has noted:

> A study conducted by Barbara Gilbert with 149 United Church of Christ clergy mainly in Massachusetts and Iowa, showed seventy-six percent of the clergy indicated they felt clergy are often isolated and have difficulty finding friends for support for personal issues. Seventy-eight percent of clergy spouses indicated they felt that clergy spouses had a difficult time finding support for dealing with personal issues. Respondents (both clergy and spouses) further indicated clergy are hesitant to ask for help when they need it (Clergy 87%, 84% spouses).[8]

In ministry we often feel like Adrian Monk from the TV show *Monk*: no matter how much we try to fit in, at the end of the day, we know that we are somehow different. We live in an isolated world in which even our closest friends may turn upon us suddenly and viciously. It does not take a person fresh out of seminary long to learn to be guarded in relationships. We enter ministry excited about serving people, and even though seasoned veterans warned us of the dangers of forming any close relationships, we soon become personal friends with someone in the

---

[8] Joel P. Sturtevant, "Confessions of a Lone Minister: Clergy Support," *Review and Expositor* 98, no. 4 (2001): 581.

church, a person that we feel we can confide in. However, it only takes one betrayal to begin to harden our hearts towards friendship. In the midst of some disagreement within the church over some policy, the person who we thought to be our confidant betrays our trust in a quest to push his or her agenda. Consequently, we retreat into the fortress of our cynicism and mistrust, vowing never to become vulnerable again.

But this sense of isolation and loneliness is not just felt by the pastor but by the whole family. The spouse is always "the pastor's wife" and the children are always "PKs" and expected to live differently than the rest of the young people in the church. When writing to Timothy, Paul expressed the loneliness that comes because of rejection. In 2 Timothy 4:10 Paul mentions that Demas had abandoned both him and the ministry. In verse 16 he further reveals the pain and isolation that he had experienced when he writes, "At my first defense no one supported me, but all deserted me; may it not be counted against them." Paul experienced further isolation when others, who were with him, left to pursue different ministries. It is no wonder that Paul passionately says to that Timothy, "Make every effort to come to me soon" (v. 9). Ministry often brings isolation. Even though we are with people all the time, we often remain unconnected, never really developing any close relationships.

Loneliness compounds exponentially when you experience rejection in ministry. Because you are relationally connected with everyone, when someone leaves the church, you not only feel a sense of loss but also a sense of rejection. You take their leaving personally, feeling a sense of abandonment as people leave to go to a different church. When several families leave, then you begin to question your capabilities and calling and begin to wonder if you should not leave the church, and perhaps even the ministry.

But all this pales in comparison to the times when we are asked to leave the church. In a study conducted in 1990, one in four pastors experienced a forced termination.[9] However, pastors often lack any other network to provide support and encouragement during these times. When faced with personal attacks, we do not always have a staff to provide encouragement,

---

[9]   Stone, *Five Ministry Killers and How to Defeat Them*, 43.

and often in rural areas, we do not even have any connections with other pastors who can give us insight, comfort, and perspective. We are truly alone. While the forced resignation leaves us financially stressed, the emotional impact upon our family and ourselves is far greater.

Another factor that leaves us feeling vulnerable, isolated, and rejected is the trend away from older pastors to younger pastors. If you are over fifty, you may be regarded as past your prime, even though Scripture says the opposite (Prov. 16:31; Job 12:12). People want a young pastor with young children so that "they will attract the younger families." Once a pastor is over sixty, he is seen only as a tired has-been who is only capable of serving some out-of-the-way church. This not only wastes a minister's experience and wisdom, but it contradicts the teaching of Scripture that honors the wisdom of the aged. For those who would serve the Lord and his people in the church, the Bible calls for elders, deacons, and deaconesses to be people distinguished especially for their maturity in character and conduct. The social, cultural, and moral upheaval occurring in North America and throughout the world necessitates the voice of experienced shepherds and servants who understand the trappings of popular culture but are not controlled by past traditions. Instead of putting the older pastor "out to pasture," younger and older alike need to hear the seasoned voice of understanding, calling us back to the moral anchor of Scripture.

The Pain of Our Own Sinfulness and Feelings of Inadequacies

When people ask me about the difficulties of ministry, they often mention how difficult it must be to bear the burdens of the problems people have. It is true that you experience stress because of the hurts people face. As a shepherd we do feel the pain and anguish people experience. However, people fail to understand that our own personal weaknesses may cause us the most discouragement and inward tension.

To enter ministry is to be reminded daily of how far you fall short of the standard God established. Every time you preach a message or teach a Bible study you come face to face with your own failures. You preach knowing you have failed to apply the very message you proclaim.

You denounce sin that inwardly you struggle with. The pedestal you are placed upon further compounds this sense of personal crisis. You feel you must be perfect to be accepted by the congregation. You fear admitting that you struggle with sin, temptation, and personal failure lest the people turn against you and use your own failures as ammunition for personal assaults against you. The tragedy is, while most people would not do so, there are always distracters who readily pounce upon your personal struggles in order to undermine your position within the church.[10] You struggle because you know how much you fail, both in ministry and in the Christian life. The messiah complex, which many of us thrust upon ourselves, or others place upon us, comes in direct and painful conflict with the fact that we have spiritual "feet of clay."

But we are not alone in this personal struggle, for even as we face our inward demons, so also Paul faced his. When he wrote to a young pastor, Paul indirectly implied to Timothy the danger of failing to recognize our own weaknesses when he said, "It is a trustworthy statement, deserving full acceptance, that Christ Jesus came into the world to save sinners, among whom I am foremost of all" (1 Tim. 1:15). In verse 13, Paul referred to his past sins, but here he uses the present tense, "I am," to refer to the continual battle he had with the sin nature still present within him. However, just as the mercy of God covered his past unbelief (vv. 13b–14), so now the mercy of God overcomes his present failings as well (v. 16). But this was more than just a candid statement of Paul's continual wrestle with sin. It served to provide a lesson to Timothy that no one is perfect, including the very people entrusted to lead the congregation. Therefore, we must live with the constant awareness that even as we proclaim the Scriptures, we are equally in need of the Scripture's instruction to us.

---

[10] For further discussion on dealing with these individuals, see Guy Greenfield, *The Wounded Minister: Healing from and Preventing Personal Attacks* (Grand Rapids: Baker Books, 2001); and Kenneth C. Haugk, *Antagonists in the Church: How to Identify and Deal with Destructive Conflict* (Minneapolis: Augsburg, 1988).

Nor did Paul escape those who would use his shortcomings to personally attack him. Some in Corinth quickly seized upon Paul's weaknesses (both personal and spiritual) in order to undermine his ministry (1 Cor. 2:3–4). However, rather than Paul allowing this to become a distraction in ministry, he instead placed himself in the hands of God and allowed God to be his judge rather than others (4:3–4). Paul points to the importance of a balanced perspective of ourselves in ministry. On the one hand, we remain flawed, broken individuals who do not stand above the congregation in the war with sin, but along with them. On the other hand, we cannot allow our sinfulness to become a distraction in our ministry to the point that we become paralyzed by the awareness of our own failures; that would lead to a sense of failure as well as inadequacy in ministry. How can we stand before others each Sunday and yet remain so flawed? While others believe that we serve as the model Christian, in many ways we know that it is a false image.

Edward Goodrick captured this tension when he penned this poem:

> I, Vessel, tarnished here and there
> By worldliness, by want of prayer
> Here in my darkened corner stand
> Unfit for use by thy clean hand
> But wait, thy cleansing touch I feel
> My shallow brim you fill with meal
> Some longing, hungry soul in need
> My unkept self, you use to feed
> Oh, wondrous grace, how can it be
> That thou canst use the likes of me.[11]

Sometimes in our sinfulness we wonder if God's grace can truly cover our failures and if we are not only unworthy of his use, but disqualified from ministry. We live a life of tension between the sufficiency of Christ and the inward sense of failure and inadequacy.

---

[11] Edward W. Goodrick, "The Likes of Me," unpublished poem. Used with permission. Dr. Goodrick was a professor for many years at Multnomah School of the Bible.

The Pain of Uncertainty and Difficulty of Knowing God's Will

We face constant pressure to lead the church in spiritual and numerical growth. We desire to effectively lead the congregation, and we are never satisfied with the present condition of the body. Because we minister in a fallen world, dealing with people plagued by sin, we never (nor should we) become fully content with the health of the church. People need to be constantly challenged to grow deeper in their relationship with God. There are always more individuals within the community who need to respond to the gospel message. The problem is never in identifying the needs. Rather, we remain perplexed on how to address the needs and move people to where they need to go. The struggle we face is not "Where does the church need to go?" but "How do we get there?" The plethora of options and programs assaulting us daily in the latest article or book, each promising success and results, only serves to further confuse us.

Ministry becomes a Rubik's cube that seems unsolvable. This riddle is compounded by the limited availability of volunteers, volunteer hours, facilities, and finances. As a result, we need to carefully discern what the church is to focus upon. The danger of any church is that it attempts to be the mini-megachurch, offering all the ministries and services of a larger congregation. Instead of bringing growth and success, people experience both burnout and ineffectiveness. It is better to do a few things well than attempt to do a number of things haphazardly. However, we often toil to discern what are the important ministries we should focus upon. We desire to know God's will for the church, but often we cannot clearly determine the specifics of what his will is. This becomes more acute when the church is facing struggles and difficulties. If only we could have clear direction. We desire to do nothing more than follow God's plan but face the difficulty of identifying that plan. Instead of it being clear, it seems illusive and unknowable. This brings confusion and paralysis in decision-making. How can we take action when we do not know what we should do?

Our drive to be successful only results in being driven by fads rather than Scripture. It seems every year a new program comes out promising that it will radically and dramatically transform our church and ministry. They promise us that our church will double in size. We continually look to the latest trend to provide the answers for ministry. But over and over again we experience disappointment and discouragement, thinking that somehow the problem must be our own failure to be like the men of Issachar "who understood the times, with knowledge of what Israel should do" (1 Chron. 12:32). We hear of others who have a clear focus of what the church should do, but find our own vision blurry and filled with uncertainty. If we were just smarter, more discerning, more insightful, then the church would grow.

The Pain of Personal Sufferings and Feelings of Vulnerability

In Numbers 20, Moses and Aaron were facing another crisis with the people. Because the Israelites lacked water, they assembled themselves against Moses and Aaron. The people challenged their leadership and questioned the promises that God had given them through Moses that he would lead them into a land filled with unending bounty. As a result, God told Moses to speak to the rock in the presence of the Israelites in order that water might come forth and God might be glorified. However, tragically, Moses took matters into his own hand, and instead of speaking to the rock, he twice struck the rock (vv. 8–11). Although God still provided water for the people, he brought a scathing rebuke against Moses. The failure that seemed so trivial was an act of unbelief and a failure to exalt God in the presence of Israel. The result was catastrophic for Moses. Because of his act of rebellion, he was not allowed to enter into the Promised Land with Israel (v. 12).

The intriguing question is, "Why did Moses do such a rash act when he had been previously faithful?" The events leading up to this tragedy should not escape our notice. In verse 1, Miriam had died and was buried. But instead of the people comforting Moses and Aaron, they grumbled against them. It is no wonder that Moses acted so angrily. When going through times of personal pain, you become vulnerable to temptation. The tragedy of these events was not only the failure of

Moses to properly give God the glory, but also the failure of the people to minister to Moses in his time of personal crisis. You spend your life ministering to the personal pain of others, but may have no one to minister to you in your times of trials. You weep in silence without the benefit of having someone comfort you. You deal with areas of temptation in silence without seeking help from others because of the fear of personal rejection. Consequently, you stand alone in your personal pain. This attempt to stand alone causes many pastors to become most vulnerable to temptation, depression, and discouragement. We do not have someone to pastor us, to help us in our brokenness.

THE RESULT OF SUFFERING

Once again we must realize in our suffering that affliction is a part of ministry. While the extent and cause of distress differs widely between each individual, each one of will face grief and pain leading to inward tears. This anguish may be external, brought on by the actions of others or by the circumstances we face that cause us to become discouraged. Perhaps, the greatest agony we face comes from within, the internal battles and struggles we face that result in discouragement and a desire to abandon the ministry.

This leads us to our crisis. Whether we consciously acknowledge it or not, the truth remains that we view suffering as something to avoid and something that should not be a part of our personal experience. When we suffer (or so we reason) it indicates that we are failures both on a personal level and on a ministerial level. But the crisis goes beyond just a personal level and taps at the heart of our relationship with God. No one ever doubts God because they are experiencing positive events in their life and apparent blessings (although God does warn us that prosperity can cause us to forget God). But when we suffer, it causes us to question God, his goodness, his care, and his involvement in our life. After all, if God were truly affirming our ministry, we would not have all the problems we experience.

While we would never verbalize such a theology, we affirm it over and over again at pastor's conferences and denominational meetings. When it comes time for testimonies, people only share how God has blessed their ministry (usually numerically) and their life (with financial blessings). No one ever stands up and gives thanks for the agony, conflicts, and problems we face. While not intentional, these testimonials imply that only the good things that happen indicate God's approval. Conversely, and more tragically, they also imply that if things are not going well, then it is because we are either doing something wrong or God is not necessarily good. The result of this is catastrophic for pastors. The average tenure of pastors is only 3.8 years, and only about one in ten pastors who start ministry in their twenties will still be in ministry when they retire at sixty-five. Perhaps the problem lies not in us or God, but in our understanding of the very nature of our call.

The question then is not will you suffer in ministry, but how will you respond to the things that cause you to become stressed? In our attempt to deal with the struggles, we focus upon dealing with the symptoms rather than the cure. We become discouraged by the circumstances we face, so we seek to change the circumstances. When we become discouraged because of the lack of growth, we leave the church in search of a better congregation only to find the same problems. Consequently, our pastorates become marked by short tenures.

When you are confronted with conflict, you can become bitter towards people for causing the inward pain you experience. When you serve in a forgotten church in a forgotten, out-of-the-way location, unrecognized by your peers and feeling abandoned by your denomination, you may drudgingly go about your duties, dreaming of a day when you will be the one recognized at the next pastor's conference for your effectiveness and innovative ministries. In our desire to avoid the pain of ministry, we become paralyzed by it. Our goal of avoiding discomfort inevitably leads to compromise, for we fear taking a stand for truth lest we come under criticism and attack. It silences us from speaking boldly the truth of God, knowing that we face difficulty, criticism, and pain. We become motivational speakers rather than biblical preachers.

Motivational speakers "leave people encouraged" in their emotions and in their "self-esteem." Biblical preaching builds up Christians in the gospel as the Holy Spirit applies the Scriptures to the hearts and minds of the hearers.[12] Motivational speakers desire to make people feel good about themselves; biblical preaching challenges people to be good.

Ministry is never easy. By its very nature it is hard and painful. To present the gospel to a lost world is to risk being labeled a fool. Preaching does not seek to merely affirm people; it seeks to radically transform people, to confront them with their sin and a faulty worldview. It is a messy business. People naturally love darkness not light and resent those who expose their sinfulness. When you challenge people's thinking and conduct, you are conducting surgery on the soul and challenging their core values and beliefs. As a result they see it as an attack on their very identity. They will take your preaching as a personal affront. They resent your intrusion into their personal life and the assumptions that they live by. But this is the task that God has called shepherds to do.

When confronted with the challenges and pain of ministry, what is needed is not a change in ministry, location, or circumstances, but a change in our understanding of God and ministry itself. What enables us to properly respond to the challenges is our theology of God, the church, and ministry itself. In the struggles we face, we need to have a right perspective, for it is in our theology that we find the answers. It is our theology, that is both believed and lived, where we find, as Paul did, the key to being content in "whatever circumstances I am. I know how to get along with humble means, and I also know how to live in prosperity; in any and every circumstance I have learned the secret of being filled and going hungry, both of having abundance and suffering need" (Phil. 4:11–12). It is what we believe about God and ministry that

---

[12] Dan Delzell, "Differences between Motivational Speaking and Biblical Preaching," *Christian Post*, September 28, 2012, accessed January 15, 2015, http://www.christianpost.com/news/differences-between-motivational-speaking-and-biblical-preaching-81902/.

enables us to continue to march boldly forward no matter how challenging the circumstances.

The problem is that even as we know these things, suffering clouds our perspective. To walk on the path of suffering is to be confronted with uncertainty, confusion, and bitterness that cause us to soon lose our way. When you started on the journey of growing in Christ, the path towards maturity was clearly visible. But in your suffering it soon becomes lost in the tangle of fear and discouragement. To find your way you need to have directions. You need an arrow to point the way. However, discovering the right signpost to guide us on our journey is not always as easy as we first think. We can easily be misled. Where do we turn to find answers? To turn to the wrong guide results in the blind leading the blind. We must learn from those who walked the same path but discovered the way to joyous contentment—weeping prophets and apostles such as Jeremiah and Paul, whom we will consider in the next chapter.

3

Regaining a Perspective of Suffering

UNDERSTANDING ITS REDEMPTIVE PURPOSE

When we think of people in the Scriptures who endured suffering, we remember the prophets and other servants of the Lord in the Old Testament, and the apostles and other disciples of Jesus in the New Testament. For Jeremiah, the joyous call to his prophetic office in the seventh century BC soon degenerated into a wail of discouragement. In chapter 1 Jeremiah received the astonishing blessing of God specifically choosing him for the special privilege of being one of his prophetic spokesmen. We can only imagine the thrill that must have pulsated through Jeremiah's heart and mind when he heard God declare that even before Jeremiah was born, God selected him to proclaim his message. Much like Timothy in the New Testament, Jeremiah initially responded with apprehension because he felt unqualified for such a high calling in view of his youth (perhaps as young as twenty). But he received the assurance that he would be empowered by God to speak his words boldly. For the next forty years, God used Jeremiah as his chief spokesman in proclaiming his message to the rebellious nation of Israel.

When Jeremiah began his ministry, there was little reason to doubt that he would experience anything but success in his work. Josiah the king, with the assistance of Hilkiah the high priest, led the southern kingdom of Judah into a period of spiritual revival and political peace. While the northern tribes of Israel had already gone into captivity because of their sin, the southern tribes of Judah were experiencing a time of economic, political, and religious prosperity. From all outward appearances, things could not be going better. According to 2 Kings 23:25, Josiah was unequaled in his faithfulness to God. Seeing the political and spiritual leadership of Josiah, Jeremiah probably was fairly confident that his prophetic leadership would be received with joy and acceptance.

It comes as no surprise to us that when things turned against him, Jeremiah cried out, "O LORD, You have deceived me and I was deceived . . . for each time I speak, I cry aloud; I proclaim violence and destruction, because for me the word of the LORD has resulted in reproach and derision all day long" (Jer. 20:7–8). What Jeremiah thought would be a well-received ministry of pronouncing blessing and joy turned into the proclamation of judgment and desolation, provoking constant ridicule. In the face of his trials, Jeremiah, like Job, cursed the day of his birth (v. 14) and wondered what the point of his life was if he was only to experience trouble and suffering (vv. 17–18).

In response God challenged Jeremiah to stand firm in the face of the trials he faced. With the equivalent to "if you can't stand the heat, stay out of the kitchen," God confronted Jeremiah, "If you have run with footmen and they have tired you out, then how can you compete with horses? If you fall down in a land of peace, how will you do in the thicket of the Jordan" (12:5). God reminded Jeremiah that if he was going to survive, he needed to maintain a right perspective of the suffering he faced. Jeremiah thought that when he became a prophet he would attain a position of honor in the land of Israel. Instead, he became a laughingstock when the message given to him by God proved to be unpopular. What Jeremiah thought would be a message of prosperity and peace turned into a message of violence and destruction. As a result people rejected both him and his message, ridiculing him for being negative and condemning (20:8). But when he tried to keep silent or conform his message to the wishes of the people, he found that the inward burning of the Spirit did not allow him to do so (v. 9).

Like Jeremiah, we increasingly face the pressure to conform our message to the world in which we live. For many even within the church, morality and truth is determined by popular culture and opinion rather than the inerrant truth of Scripture. We redefine and re-interpret Scripture to coincide with the modern view of morality and truth rather than submit to biblical authority. Yet it should not escape our notice that God warns the people against prophets who only say what they want to hear, who fail to warn against calamity and judgment (23:16–17).

What the church needs today are Jeremiahs—preachers who confront sin and warn of judgment rather than preachers who just proclaim peace and prosperity. But to do so will be costly, even as it was for Jeremiah. Yet the mark of a true shepherd is courage rather than fear (23:4). We must be willing to be like Jeremiah who faced the threat of death by the priests and other prophets when his message did not correspond to their desires (26:7–24), who continued to record the prophecies of God even after they burned them (36:20–32), and who was willing to be thrown into the muck of a pit rather than compromise his message (38:1–6).

The lament and complaint of Jeremiah resonates with us. When we enter ministry, we anticipate assaulting the gates of hell and seeing the enemy tremble in response (Matt. 16:18–20). However, the longer we stay in ministry the more we see ourselves caught in spiritual trench warfare. We daily see the slaughter on the battlefield, but nothing seems to be gained. Like Jeremiah we begin to wonder, what is the point? If this is all we see accomplished, then is it really worth the pain? However, the problem is not the lack of success but our failure to understand the purpose of suffering. Because we have a negative view of suffering, we cannot see how God accomplishes his purpose through it. As we examine the pages of Scripture we find a different perspective. We assume that if we strive to accomplish something good for the kingdom, then the outcomes will always be pleasant. Older voices may have told us otherwise, but the energy and enthusiasm of youth and idealism tend to make it hard to really hear and receive such wisdom. We now recognize that discouragement comes from life in the trenches, but shouldn't the outcome be both positive and pleasant? When it is not, we question the validity of our acts.

SUFFERING AND THE CALL TO MINISTRY

Recently we conducted a survey of our congregation in order to assess the general attitude of the people and how we might improve our church. While many responses were positive, there were some that were highly critical and several that even suggested it was now time for a change in the pastoral leadership. As we go about the day, we expect to have some challenges. What we do not anticipate is the severity of the attacks. It is one thing when people criticize a program or decision; it is another when they call for your resignation.

Stephen Ambrose, in his book *Band of Brothers*, recounts the three stages a combat soldier goes through on the battlefield when faced with the reality of death: "it *can't* happen to me, then it *can* happen to me," and finally "it is *going* to happen to me."[1] We often experience the same thing. When we first entered ministry, we heard stories of pastors being fired for trivial reasons but felt secure, reasoning that we are more skilled in our leadership and better trained. But the longer we remain in the trenches, the more we begin to realize that personal attacks against us can and will happen. We soon realize, along with Paul that ministry brings us to the trenches of spiritual warfare where we fight against spiritual forces of darkness. We soon realize the battlefield is not a safe place. It is a place of destruction and attack, where ground is gained at an incredible cost to those engaged in the conflict. When Paul exhorts us in Ephesians 6 to put on the full armor of God and to stand firm, the implication is obvious—we face certain attack and constant risk of spiritual injury.

In Matthew 5:10–12, Jesus warns his disciples of the reality of persecution and suffering in ministry: "Blessed are those who have been persecuted for the sake of righteousness, for theirs is the kingdom of heaven. Blessed are you when people insult you and persecute you, and falsely say all kinds of evil against you because of Me. Rejoice and

---

[1]   Stephen E. Ambrose, *Band of Brothers: E Company, 506th Regiment, 101st Airborne; from Normandy to Hitler's Eagle's Nest* (New York: Simon & Schuster, 1992), 154.

be glad, for your reward in heaven is great; for in the same way they persecuted the prophets who were before you." The gospel inherently offends a world of people embracing their sin (John 3:19–21). The message of Christ is foolishness to them (1 Cor. 1:18–25). Consequently, Jesus warns us that persecution will be part of our identification with him: "Blessed are those who have been persecuted for the sake of righteousness." Concerning the verb "persecuted" in Matthew 5:10, pastor-teacher John MacArthur writes, "The Greek verb is a passive perfect participle, and could be translated 'allow themselves to be persecuted.' The perfect form indicates continuousness, in this case a continuous willingness to endure persecution if it is the price of godly living. This beatitude speaks of a constant attitude of accepting whatever faithfulness to Christ may bring."[2] To live for Christ and proclaim his message risks facing rejection from people who denounce Christ and so reject his followers. The term "insult" in verse 11 refers to the mocking and verbal abuse confronting followers of Jesus. It refers to speaking disparagingly of another in a manner that is not justified.[3]

To respond properly, we must recognize that just as people directed hatred towards the prophets of old, so we will face the same response. But rather than shrink back in fear, Jesus challenges us to "rejoice and be glad" (v. 12), which Bible scholar John Nolland says is "to recognize one's good fortune. The call is to experience the present in the immediate connection with the ultimate outcome in the kingdom of heaven."[4] In other words, rather than seeing the personal attacks against us as harmful, we rejoice, knowing that even in the midst of our persecution, God achieves his purposes in and through us. Rather than the attack

---

[2] John MacArthur Jr., *Matthew 1–7*, MacArthur New Testament Commentary (Chicago: Moody, 1985), 224.

[3] Johannes P. Louw and Eugene A. Nida, *Greek-English Lexicon of the New Testament: Based on Semantic Domains*, electronic ed. of the 2nd ed., 2 vols. (New York: United Bible Societies, 1996), 1:432.

[4] John Nolland, *The Gospel of Matthew: A Commentary on the Greek Text*, New International Greek Testament Commentary (Grand Rapids: Eerdmans, 2005), 209.

thwarting God's plan, he uses the persecution we face to further establish his kingdom.

The greatest tragedy is not the suffering we experience, but the concealment of our faith or the compromise of our message in order to avoid the rejection of the world. Nolland summarizes our need to resist temptation on both sides: "Persecution for righteousness' sake is to be set over against compromise and apostasy; it marks fidelity to God despite all kinds of pressure."[5] In response to the threat of concealing our message, Jesus encourages us to remain all the more visible, like a light placed on a stand to give light to all those who come in contact with it (Matt. 5:14–16). Instead of concealing the fact that we are disciples of Christ, we are to boldly proclaim our allegiance through word and action. However, in doing so we recognize that persecution is part of discipleship (and by implication, ministry) and part of living for Christ (John 15:18–21). When we accept Christ, we enter a spiritual battlefield where we will face opposition and personal attack. "It is *going* to happen to me."

SUFFERING AND THE LIFE OF FAITH

The prophet Jeremiah had to come to terms with the reality that his faithful preaching of the message God gave him caused him personal pain and suffering. The apostle Paul took it a step further when he pointed out that our identification with Christ results in suffering. In Romans 8:16–18, Paul writes that "the Spirit Himself testifies with our spirit that we are children of God, and if children, heirs also, heirs of God and fellow heirs with Christ, if indeed we suffer with Him so that we may also be glorified with Him. For I consider that the sufferings of this present time are not worthy to be compared with the glory that is to be revealed to us." Paul argues that if we are heirs of God and partakers in the inheritance that Christ receives, then it follows that we must also be partakers in his suffering. The construction of the conditional

---

[5]   Ibid., 206.

clause "if indeed we suffer with Him" assumes this reality will be true. Facing persecution and trials does not exist in the realm of possibility, but of certainty. By making the clause conditional, Paul does not question the possibility of suffering. He only raises the question of when it will occur. New Testament scholar James Dunn clarifies the implications of the text: "Yet they will enjoy that full inheritance (in the future) only if their identification with Christ goes all the way, not simply with his lifestyle on earth or in experience of his risen life already, but also in sharing of his sufferings and death."[6]

We often believe that when we live for Christ our lives should be comfortable and free from problems. In this we (like Jeremiah) are seriously mistaken. Paul rather argues that trials and opposition inevitably come because of our faith. However, rather than this being destructive, for Paul the hostility reveals the genuineness of our faith as we respond with trust and hope in Christ. If the followers of Jesus in general face persecution, how much more will it be true of those leading the church? If Satan opposes Christians and strives to defeat them through adversity, he will seek to destroy those who lead the congregation, for if he destroys the shepherd he will destroy the flock as well. Puritan pastor Richard Baxter warns fellow ministers, "Take heed to yourselves because the tempter will make his first and sharpest assault on you. If you will be leaders against him, he will not spare you. He bears the greatest malice against the man who is engaged in working the greatest damage against him."[7]

Privileged to Suffer for Christ's Sake

God has given us the greatest privilege of being co-heirs with Christ (Gal. 4:7), not that we just share the eternal inheritance that God gives

---

[6]   James D. G. Dunn, *Romans 1–8*, Word Biblical Commentary 38A (Nashville: Thomas Nelson, 1988), 423.

[7]   Richard Baxter, *The Reformed Pastor: A Pattern for Personal Growth and Ministry*, ed. James M. Houston (Portland: Multnomah, 1982), 35–36.

his son, but that he imputes the character and righteousness of Christ upon us (3:27). He accomplished far more than merely redeeming us from the clutches of sin's judgment; he instilled his life in us so that we now have eternal life (2:20). Consequently, rather than shrinking back from such persecution, Paul, in Philippians 1:29, challenges us to bear it as a privilege.

In the previous verses, in light of the persecution brought upon them by their opponents, Paul exhorts his readers to conduct themselves in a manner worthy of the gospel (v. 27). In the face of such attacks, we must stand firm in our faith, and in verse 29 he gives the reason why we should take such a positive view towards suffering: "For to you it has been granted for Christ's sake, not only to believe in Him, but also to suffer for His sake." New Testament scholar Peter O'Brien offers additional perspective: "In a surprising statement Paul explains why the present situation of the Philippians is a sign of their future salvation: it is because their believing in Christ and especially their suffering for his sake has been 'graciously given' to them by God."[8]

Moreover, in verse 29 the term "granted" means "to give or grant graciously and generously, with the implication of good will on the part of the giver."[9] Bible scholar Marvin Vincent explains further: "The word is significant as opening the conception of suffering from the Christian point of view. God rewards and endorses believers with the gift of suffering."[10] Just as our salvation expresses God's gracious gift to us, so also enduring hardships for him reveals his grace, for it serves as a testimony to our identification with Christ and his sufferings (see also 2 Tim. 3:12).

---

[8]   Peter T. O'Brien, *The Epistle to the Philippians: A Commentary on the Greek Text*, New International Greek Testament Commentary (Grand Rapids: Eerdmans, 1991), 158.

[9]   Louw and Nida, *Greek-English Lexicon of the New Testament*, 1:568.

[10]   Marvin R. Vincent, *A Critical and Exegetical Commentary on the Epistles to the Philippians and to Philemon*, International Critical Commentary, (Edinburgh: T&T Clark, 1985), 35.

Paul puts in parallel the grace of God revealed in our salvation and the privilege to suffer for his sake. This is why in 2 Corinthians 12:10 he states, "Therefore I am well content with weaknesses, with insults, with distresses, with persecutions, with difficulties, for Christ's sake; for when I am weak, then I am strong." The suffering you encounter does not defeat you. Rather, it makes you stronger because it serves as a reminder that you do not conduct ministry by your own intellectual prowess and organizational abilities but by the power of God. Rather than suffering being a mark of shame, it becomes a mark of honor, bearing testimony to your relationship with Christ.

Called to Suffer as the Lord's Servants

In Colossians 1:24, Paul makes a statement that at first glance perplexes us: "Now I rejoice in my sufferings for your sake, and in my flesh I do my share on behalf of His body, which is the church, in filling up what is lacking in Christ's affliction." The statement that Paul rejoices in his sufferings should not surprise us, because we have already seen why he found joy in suffering for Christ. What is perplexing in this verse is his statement that his suffering fills up what is lacking in Christ's affliction. The verb translated "do my share . . . in filling up" is a rare double compound of the verb "to fill" formed with the two prepositions "up" and "in turn." Concerning this verb, Robertson writes, "It is now Paul's 'turn' at the bat, to use a baseball figure. Christ had his 'turn,' the grandest of all and suffered for us all in a sense not true of anyone else."[11] When the world vented its hatred towards Christ on the cross, that hatred was not fully satiated. Because Christ is no longer present to receive the outpouring of their hatred, they now turn their wrath toward his followers (see also Gal. 6:17; 2 Cor. 1:5; Phil. 3:10).[12]

---

[11]   Robertson, *Word Pictures in the New Testament*, 4:484, comments on Col. 1:24.

[12]   William Hendriksen, *Philippians, Colossians and Philemon*, New Testament Commentary (Grand Rapids: Baker, 1979), 87.

But these attacks are not without cause or benefit. Paul saw his sufferings as necessary so the message of Christ might be brought to the Gentile community. Just as they shared in the benefit of Christ's death through their salvation, so now they receive the benefit of the ministry of Paul and the trials he endured because of it. However, the hatred of the world towards Christ did not end with Paul, for it continues to be directed at believers today and those who serve the church. Now it is our turn "at bat." Just as the persecution of Paul served to benefit the church, so now our ministry and the mistreatment that comes with it continues to profit the people we serve.

In 2 Timothy 1:8–12, Paul highlights this different perspective. When we experience adversity we often see it as a hindrance—how can we be effective when under attack? But Paul saw it differently. He saw the gospel as more powerful than the opposition he faced. For Paul, the gospel transcends suffering, and the gospel displays its true power in the context of trials. The hostility he faced was not a veil concealing the gospel. Rather, it served as the backdrop to highlight the true nature of the gospel.

Through our suffering, the gospel of Christ is communicated. If opposition is an intrinsic part of proclaiming Christ, then we must recognize that we cannot be involved in ministry without any personal cost. If we abandon the pastorate because of suffering rather than following God's direction in our life and ministry, then the benefit that would have been to the church is lost. Certainly, there are occasions when God moves people out of pastoral ministry and into new areas of service. When this happens, we recognize that God has another and equally important role for us to play in his redemptive plan. Like an athlete who needs to head to the bench for a period of rest and recuperation before rejoining the fray, there may be times where we need to step away from ministry to be physically, emotionally, and spiritually rejuvenated so we can be effective in our service. But when we permanently check out from all forms of ministry because we have surrendered to the pressures, we negate the power of the gospel working through us.

The power of the gospel is revealed in our weakness, especially when we realize our inabilities and trust in his empowerment. The power of the gospel enables us to see beyond the present suffering and the glory that is to be revealed to us (Rom. 8:18–25). It is in our suffering that our hope in Christ is placed on full display for the world to see.

SUFFERING AND GOD'S TRANSFORMATIONAL PURPOSE

Suffering is not arbitrary nor is it merely a result of the spiritual battle we are in as though we face affliction only because of Satan's intent to demolish and demoralize believers in general and church leaders in particular. God's sovereignty works not only to protect believers from facing more than they can handle (1 Cor. 10:13), but also to orchestrate the trials in such a way that they achieve his transformational purpose in our lives and lives of others. Isn't it true that you often view the events that happen in your life from a temporal perspective? You evaluate the circumstances in your life by the effect that it has upon your present attitudes and actions. When you face trials, you only see the destructive effects because you only see it from the context of the present. When forced to leave a church, you cannot see how it has any positive effect in your life or in the lives of the people you serve. How can there be any benefit when malicious gossips and vicious individuals more concerned about protecting their own turf than building the kingdom of God have torpedoed your ministry? What you do not see, nor can you see, is how God weaves the pain you experience into his eternal plan leading to you own spiritual growth and the salvation of others.

But we are not left in the dark to aimlessly search for purpose or meaning behind the tragic events that seem to strike us without any rhyme or reason. Instead, we find that even in the midst of our most difficult circumstances, God accomplishes his purpose though us. God's purpose in our life cannot be thwarted by the destructive actions of others. This lesson was understood by Joseph when he looked back upon the ill treatment he received at the hands of his brothers. Rather than become bitter at their evil plans, he instead placed their actions in the context of God's purpose and plans: "As for you, you meant evil against me, but God meant it for good in order to bring about this present result, to preserve many people alive" (Gen. 50:20).

Shortly before his death in a Gestapo prison, Dietrich Bonhoeffer, one who understood the cost of following Christ and the personal pain it brings, wrote a letter to his fiancée, Maria, around Christmas 1944. It was his last letter to her. In it he references a nineteenth-century German writer and poet Adalbert Stifter.

> Stifter once said, "pain is a holy angel, who shows treasures to men which otherwise remain forever hidden; through him men have become greater than through all the joys of the world." It must be so and I tell this to myself in my present position over and over again—the pain of longing which often can be felt even physically, must be there, and we shall not, and need not, talk it away. But it needs to be overcome every time and thus there is an even holier angel than the one of pain, that is the one of the joy in God.[13]

Suffering is more than just something we must endure. It is our teacher that God uses to mold and shape us. Through the lesson of suffering, we often learn the most about ourselves and the God we serve.

GOD'S REDEMPTIVE PURPOSE IN SUFFERING

When we examine the sufferings of Christ, we easily understand the purpose they served. Not only did the Old Testament foretell his beatings and death, the whole of Scripture shows the necessity of it for our redemption. Without the sufferings of Christ, no one would have eternal life. While we readily see the correlation between Christ's suffering and God's redemptive plan, we often cannot see how suffering relates

---

13 Quoted in Eric Metaxas, *Bonhoeffer: Pastor, Martyr, Prophet, Spy; A Righteous Gentile vs. the Third Reich* (Nashville: Thomas Nelson, 2010), 495.

to us. Yet Paul saw his personal anguish not only as a part of his identification with Christ but also part of God's redemptive work that God accomplished through Christ in the lives of people (Col. 1: 24; 2 Cor. 4:8–12). But Paul not only affirmed these truths in his theology, he realized them in his life. He lived in the trenches, and he knew firsthand the full cost of being in ministry. Almost every trial we face, Paul fully identified with, whether that be rejection, criticism, inward anxiety, or full-fledged persecution (2 Cor. 11:22–33). Yet, through his personal experience and understanding of God's activity he gained a perspective that enabled him to see his suffering achieving eternal results, not only in his life, but also in the lives of others.

In Acts 16:22–40, we find Paul and Silas in the one place where no one would want to be: in a dark, damp Roman prison, feet fastened in stocks, recovering from fresh wounds obtained by a brutal beating inflicted by the Romans. At first glance, it appears the opposition won. Instead of the people rejoicing in a young woman's deliverance from demonic possession (vv. 16–18), they had turned against Paul and Silas. Tragically, the owner of the servant girl revealed a cold-hearted lack of concern for this young girl. Instead of rejoicing in her healing, he only lamented his loss of profit (vv. 19–21). Like a board member who viscously turns upon you when he loses power in the church, so the master stirred up the crowds against Paul and Silas. As a result, they found themselves badly beaten up and in prison.

The opposition had silenced the witness and preaching of Paul. However, Paul had refrained from mentioning something—that he was a Roman citizen (v. 37)! And this would have insulated him from false arrest and beating. Why Paul did not mention his citizenship until the next morning we can only guess. Perhaps in the shock and upheaval of the events, Paul completely forgot to mention it (unlikely). Perhaps Paul trusted that God had a greater purpose and he was going to wait to see what it was (more probable). Whatever, the reason for Paul's silence, Paul was not sitting in the throes of despair because of his circumstances. Instead, he trusted in God's sovereign work in his life and ministry.

Paul and Silas, in spite of their circumstances, revealed their complete trust in God by two astonishing acts. First, instead of groveling in frustration and anger that God allowed such a thing to happen, they sang praises to God, trusting in his deliverance, and using the opportunity to be a witness to others (v. 25). It is one thing to sing songs of praise when life is pleasant; it is quite another to do so when life is harsh and painful. Second, even when the opportunity arose for them to flee, they calmly waited, trusting that God had a greater purpose to achieve than just their deliverance (vv. 26–28).

While Paul and Silas did not have the opportunity at the time to understand the purpose behind their distress, as we read the narrative we have the privilege of seeing the end result. What must have seemed to them like a traumatic turn of events was God orchestrating the affair to provide an opportunity for Christ to be manifested through them in such a way that the jailer came to realize the grace and forgiveness of Christ (vv. 26–34). While the text does not say exactly what caused his sudden conversion, there were a number of things that could have influenced his decision. Certainly fear, not only of the earthquake but also the certainty of his death if the prisoners escaped, strongly impacted him. It must have been shocking for him when the prisoners, under the influence of Paul and Silas, remained in their cells even when presented with the opportunity to flee. Such an act of grace would have caused the jailer to see that Paul and Silas were vastly different from the normal vagabonds that populated his cells. Whatever went through his mind in those minutes that transpired, it was enough to make him realize that Paul and Silas were indeed witnesses and followers of the true God.

But it is in this story that we find a critical principle of suffering. We often view suffering, especially in the form of opposition and personal attack, to be a threat to our personal well-being and ministry. However, what we view to be a threat to God's work in our ministry provides an opportunity for God to manifest his power and strength through us.

Hosea likewise illustrates this when God commanded him to marry Gomer, an adulterer (see Hosea 1–3). Concerning the pain experienced by Hosea, pastor and Bible teacher James Montgomery Boice writes, "We live in an age where everything good is interpreted in terms of happiness and success. So when we think of spiritual blessings, we think of it in these terms. To be led of God and be blessed by God means that we will be 'happy' and 'successful.' . . . This is shallow thinking and shallow Christianity, for God does not always lead His people into ways that we would naturally regard as happy or as filled with success." Boice goes on to say, "Let us put this down as a great principle: God sometimes leads His children to do things that afterwards involve them in great distress. But because God does not think as we think or act as we act, it is often in these situations that He accomplishes His greatest victories and brings the greatest blessing to His name."[14] While we may not always understand the purpose and benefit of our suffering, we must trust that God often uses our suffering to reveal his grace and redemption to a dying world.

C. S. Lewis once wrote, "God whispers to us in our pleasures, speaks in our conscience, but shouts in our pains: it is His megaphone to rouse a deaf world."[15] It may equally be said, that our pain and sorrow is often his megaphone that he uses to shout to others. It is through your pain that others often hear most clearly the reality of God's grace revealed in your life. People see the hope you have in Christ through your pain not your comfort (1 Peter 3:15). Suffering provides five invaluable lessons that serve to enhance your ministry and enable you to be more effective.

Suffering Provides Perspective

It is easy to lose perspective. While ministry has its many hardships, it also dangerously feeds the ego. People commend us for our preaching. At social events, they treat us with special honor. They look up to us for our wisdom and counsel. Creating a false image of our own spirituality,

---

[14] James Montgomery Boice, *The Minor Prophets: An Expositional Commentary*, vol. 1, *Hosea–Jonah* (Grand Rapids: Zondervan, 1983), 15.

[15] Lewis, *Problem of Pain*, 93.

people place us on a pedestal. If we are not careful, we can easily start to listen to our fan mail and gain an elevated view of ourselves. Pride is a dangerous and subtle deceiver. While on the one hand we must speak the Word of God with confidence and boldness, that confidence can easily harden into pride and arrogance. Instead of humbly pointing people to the Messiah, we start to think that we are their messiah. When we hear of other pastors going through difficulties and trials, we not only rejoice that we are not facing such troubles, but we smugly think that if they had handled the crisis better (as we would have done), they would not have faced those problems. When things go well we attribute it to our abilities and leadership skills. We start to think that somehow we are a cut above the rest.

Paul understood this temptation because he faced the same enticement in his own life. He talks about this in 2 Corinthians 12. Paul had the special privilege of gaining a glimpse into the presence of God and seeing what few humans have ever seen while still alive on this earth. Such a privilege, coupled with his calling as an apostle, could easily have resulted in Paul gaining a superior view of himself. Although he did not have the privilege of being one of the first disciples, the special calling he received and his position as the preeminent theologian in the early church placed before him the danger of viewing himself as someone special. In the early church, few could match Paul's theological training and insight. As a result, God used Paul to communicate the core passages outlining the theological foundation of the early church. Consequently, it would have been easy for Paul to begin to fall prey to the subtle danger of self-importance. In order to prevent this, God used the voice of suffering to keep Paul from becoming focused on himself rather than on the grace of God operating through him (2 Cor. 12:7). What the proverbial "thorn in the flesh" was has been widely speculated. It may have been a physical weakness (some have suggested malaria, others poor eyesight) or it may have been a particular spiritual struggle or temptation that Paul could not gain full victory over.

Whatever it was, it caused sufficient turmoil that he asked three times for its removal. However, rather than providing Paul relief, God made it clear that it was to serve as a continual reminder that Paul was to rest in the grace of God and recognize that it is in man's weakness that God's power is most evident. As a result, rather than being angry because of his circumstances, Paul gladly embraced the struggles he faced, "Therefore I am well content with weaknesses, with insults, with distresses, with persecutions, with difficulties, for Christ's sake; for when I am weak, then I am strong" (12:10). Paul saw a direct relationship between these trials and his spiritual equilibrium. The suffering he endured continued to teach him humility so he would always remember that his effectiveness stemmed from God's activity and grace, not his own efforts.

Often we become angry when life (and people) treats us unfairly. But these things, rather than being venom that spiritually poisons our soul, serve as a catharsis purging the soul of the insidious infection of pride and arrogance. It reminds us that we can only perform our ministry by the strength and grace of God (2 Cor. 3:5; 1 Cor. 2:1–5). Rather than difficulties and adversities distorting our perspective, they serve to help maintain our spiritual equilibrium. It should not drive us from ministry, but drive us continually back to be cleansed and renewed in the grace of God so we might continually remember that we are who we are in Christ and we accomplish what we accomplish only by God's grace.

Suffering Teaches Dependency

A bedfellow of pride is self-sufficiency. We easily start to rely upon our training, our intellectual aptitude, our relational skills, and our personal talents to perform our responsibilities. Tragically, in the modern era, we have turned the church from a spiritual and confessional institution to an organizational business. The measure of success has become size, growth, budgets, and facilities. What seminary president Albert Mohler states regarding theological education may easily be said of the church: "We are living in an anti-confessional age. Our society and its reigning academic culture are committed to individual autonomy and expression, as well as to an increasingly relativistic conception of truth. The language of higher education is overwhelmingly dominated by claims of academic freedom, rather than academic responsibility. In most schools, a confession of faith is an anathema, not just an anachronism. But, among us, a confession of faith must be seen as a gift and covenant. It is a sacred trust that guards revealed truths. A confession of faith never stands above the Bible, but the Bible itself mandates concern for the pattern of sound words."[16]

Ironically, in a profession centered on faith, we have abandoned it. While we affirm theologically the absolute truth of Scripture we have rejected its sufficiency. Churches no longer stand for theological truth and clarity. We have forsaken the centrality of clear creedal statements that serve to define and govern both what we believe and how we live. Instead of affirming the importance of theology, we avoid it, seeing it as divisive, and in so doing we undermine the foundation of the church. We forsake clarity and pursue ambiguity. Consequently, we often view the strategic planner, the marketer, and business manager to have more to say to the church than the theologian and biblical scholar. Many pastors and church leaders have become more concerned about the branding and marketing of the church than the theological truth upon which it stands. When preaching, many of us are more concerned about offending people than proclaiming biblical truth. But the subtle change to a business model of church not only affects the message and focus of the church; it also changes our view of ourselves and our abilities in ministry.

Running a successful business does not require supernatural empowerment to be effective. As long as a person is driven, able to keep his or her pulse on the market, and able to identify, organize, and achieve desired goals, then a person can be successful. The focus shifts from what God does through us to what we do for God. Churches and congregations look for pastors who are visionaries, organizers, and

---

[16] Albert Mohler, "Confessional Integrity and the Stewardship of Words," AlbertMohler.com, May 1, 2013, accessed October 23, 2013, http://www.albertmohler.com/2013/05/01/confessional-integrity-and-the-stewardship-of-words/.

charismatic speakers rather than people of character and proclaimers of truth. As a result, the temptation is strong to start relying upon our organizational and interpersonal relational skills to be effective within the church. Instead of the work of the church being the mysterious activity that God does through us, it becomes something that can be manipulated by our business skills.

This self-reliance goes counter grain to the priorities of the New Testament. We are entrusted with the task of proclaiming the truth. At the end of ministry, we will be evaluated not by how successful we have been, but by how faithful we have been to proclaim the Scriptures and live in obedience to them. Our task is not to build a large organization, but to lead people in spiritual transformation (Col. 1:28–29). But this becomes lost in the business approach to ministry. Today, we assume that the size of the church indicates the effectiveness of the church. But external appearances can hide inward corruption. Just because many people attend the services each week does not mean that they are being transformed inwardly. Our task is not primarily to achieve growth in the physical realm, but the spiritual. We cannot achieve this on our own strength. It is something produced in and through us and others by the Holy Spirit.

Paul recognizes that the attempt to accomplish our mission in our own strength not only fails but diametrically opposes the very calling we received. In 1 Corinthians 2:1–5, he expressly states that he came divested of any attempt to base his ministry on his own skills and talents. Instead, he relied solely upon the power of the message itself in order that the focus might be upon Christ, rather than himself. To understand this confession we must recognize that he learned this through the struggles he faced. Trials and adversity quickly reveal our inadequacies. Paul faced every situation conceivable. He faced times of financial prosperity; he faced times when he lacked the basic needs of life. He faced persecution not only from those opposed to the gospel, but by the very people he served.

Yet Paul saw these circumstances, not as a destroyer in his life, but as a teacher. It taught him that the sufficiency of Christ, not his circumstances, governed his sense of contentment. It taught him that success was not attained through skills and talents, but by complete dependency upon the one who strengthens him to accomplish all things (Phil. 4:10–13). The suffering and trials remind us that we bring nothing to the table. We enter into the ministry divested of anything ensuring our success. Rather, we completely rely upon God's enablement both to perform the task of ministry as well as accomplish anything of eternal value.

Suffering Reveals the Genuineness of Our Faith

There are no long-term pretenders in ministry. While a person may enter with wrong motives and even a superficial faith, the trials and struggles will eventually expose the true condition and motive of the heart. It is easy to maintain the facade of spirituality when there is no cost and nothing challenges the depth of our faith. But when adversity strikes and ministry no longer gives us affirmation and prestige, what we truly believe will be revealed. This is what leads to a crisis of faith.

While Paul states unequivocally, "If God is for us, who can be against us," we often wonder, "If everyone is against us, how can God be for us?" Suffering not only causes us to doubt ourselves, it causes us to doubt God. While preaching and challenging people to stand firm in their faith, we struggle ourselves if we're honest, don't we? But the problem is not just our perception of ourselves, or even of God. The problem is our failure to understand the refining nature of suffering. It both reveals and refines our faith. As we have seen with Job, the struggles we face become the spotlight God uses to highlight the genuineness of our faith so others might be strengthened by it.

The greatest sermon God proclaims through us is not the message we proclaim in our words, but the message he reveals through our life. Peter reminds us to always be ready to give a reason for the hope that we have (1 Peter 3:15). This hope is only revealed when it is tested and shown to be genuine. It should not surprise us that this verse comes in the context of suffering for Christ (vv. 13–14). Everyone maintains a faith in something, but trials reveal the true nature of one's faith.

Genuine faith is revealed when the circumstances point to the very opposite—when the things we believe do not appear to be true. Singer-songwriter Laura Story points this out in her song "Blessings," a song written from the context of the pain of real-life trials and adversities, primarily when her husband was diagnosed with a brain tumor. One of many questions the song asks is, "And what if trials of this life, the rain, the storms, the hardest nights are Your mercies in disguise?"[17] By asking the questions she points us to the answer—that suffering is often the avenue through which God bestows his blessing upon us. Suffering is the voice that gives expression to our faith, revealing to others that what we believe is not just a set of creeds we confess, but a truth that we embrace and live.

Suffering Brings Transformation

Suffering refines our faith. It is the tool God uses to develop our character. The apostle James writes that we should rejoice in our suffering because trials develop Christlikeness in our life (James 1:2–4). If suffering is our voice to the world, then suffering is God's scalpel by which he brings healing surgery to our soul. If God desires to bring about radical transformation, then James sees suffering as the process God uses to bring about that change. Instead of seeing affliction as a tragedy, James views it at the basis for God's activity in our life. When we respond with grumbling at trials, we prohibit God from achieving his purpose.

In James' argument we see a progression. He begins with a command in verse 2 to "consider it all joy, my brethren," which implies a sense of urgency and the need to rearrange our attitude towards the trials we face. James is not merely looking at some hypothetical suffering, but the real pain that each of us will encounter at some point in the future. Knowing that God uses suffering positively in your life gives you the basis for the joy even in the midst of the struggles you

---

[17] Laura Story, "Blessings," *Blessings*, produced by Nathan Nockels (Brentwood, TN: INO Records, 2011).

encounter (v. 3). While you may not know all the reasons for the suffering, you already know the end result. Consequently, you respond with a different viewpoint. Instead of quickly abandoning your faith or ministry, you endure the trials in order that God's purpose might be fully realized (vv. 3–4).

As we have seen, suffering has a purpose in the ministry we have with others, but it also has a purpose in our own spiritual growth as well. Most parents recognize that one of the most unloving things they can do is to insulate their children from experiencing any suffering or pain. Not only does growth and development toward maturity involve suffering, but attaining happiness involves pain as well. For children to enjoy the lifelong fun of riding bikes, they must first experience the pain of scraped knees and elbows. To learn the depth of love, they must be vulnerable to experiencing the pain of rejection. To learn sportsmanship and the thrill of victory, they must endure the discomfort of running wind sprints as well as losing to a more skillful opponent or a better team. To learn the joy of attaining goals and having success, they must experience falling short and failure yet also learn from it. A loving parent does not protect a child from pain. Rather, a loving parent allows and uses the pain children experience as a tool to teach them the necessary principles and skills to prepare them for adulthood. This is equally true of God. As a loving father, not only does he discipline us, but he also allows us to go through difficult trials in order that we might become mature in Christ.

Suffering Equips Us for Ministry

God calls us to minister to broken people facing all kinds of trials and difficulties, whether they are an individual diagnosed with terminal cancer, a spouse broken because of rejection and abuse, or a person struggling with temptation and sin. The most effective minister is not one who stands on the sidelines shouting trite and hollow words of encouragement. Rather, it is the one who has experienced the pain and sorrows they face and knows firsthand the anguish they encounter.

Christ set the pattern for this when he became fully man. Not only was his incarnation important for our salvation as the substitutionary sacrifice, it was also important for his ministry to us. Christ became fully human in order that he might share our sorrows, in order that we might identify with him and he with us. He knew the hurt of rejection, the depth of temptation, the pains of hunger, and the longing of thirst. He experienced the silence of heaven and the feel of being forsaken by God. It should not escape our notice that Isaiah described him as a "man of sorrows and acquainted with grief" (Isa. 53:3). As a result, he became our sympathetic high priest, one who fully understands our weaknesses (Heb. 4:14–15).

A shepherd does not care for the sheep in the confines of a plush leather chair in a cozy office. Shepherding involves being out with the sheep, facing the same dangers, storms, and discomforts. When Christ refers to himself as the Chief Shepherd, he reveals himself as a sacrificial shepherd willingly suffering for the sheep. But what slides on the level slides downhill. If Christ experienced suffering in order to be our shepherd, we can expect no less. We become equipped for ministering to the hurts of others by experiencing the same grief in our own life (2 Cor. 1:3–4). It is one thing when someone quotes Romans 8:28 from the safety of their own ease. It is quite another when it is someone who has already gone through the same circumstances and can still testify of its truth. When we experience God's comfort in our pain, we learn how to comfort people in theirs.

Paul describes himself as an earthen vessel, a piece of pottery that is easily broken. He summarizes the afflictions he faced when he wrote,

> But we have this treasure in earthen vessels, so that the surpassing greatness of the power will be of God and not from ourselves; we are afflicted in every way, but not crushed; perplexed, but not despairing; persecuted, but not forsaken; struck down, but not destroyed; always carrying about in the body the dying of Jesus, so that the life of Jesus also may be manifested in our body. For we who live are constantly being delivered over to death for Jesus' sake, so that the life of Jesus also

may be manifested in our mortal flesh. So death works in us, but life in you. (2 Cor. 4:7–12)

Yet he saw this as a necessary part of being equipped by God to serve others. Earlier he had written to the same church in Corinth, "Blessed be the God and Father of our Lord Jesus Christ, the Father of mercies and God of all comfort, who comforts us in all our affliction so that we will be able to comfort those who are in any affliction with the comfort with which we ourselves are comforted by God" (2 Cor. 1:3–4). It is through the pain of ministry that we discover the strength of ministry. While seminary trained us theologically and biblically for ministry, it is the suffering we face that trains us how to apply those truths to ourselves and the lives of the people we serve.

REGAINING PERSPECTIVE IN THE MIDST OF SUFFERING

The psalmists were well versed in the pains of life. Their honesty as they present their laments before God captures the feelings and pains we wrestle with ourselves. But the real appeal of the Psalms stem from the unwavering confidence the writers had in the response of God to their cry. Even in the midst of the deepest anguish, the psalmists express the assurance that God will soon bring their deliverance (see, for example, Psalm 13). But we wrestle with the question, "How could the psalmists remain so confident in the face of so much hardship?" The answer lies in Psalm 119. When life pressed down upon them to the point where their soul "weeps because of grief" (v. 28), rather than abandoning themselves to the pit of despair, they turned to the pages of Scripture. Over and over again, the psalmist in Psalm 119 sees the Scriptures as the source of his comfort and revival:

> My soul cleaves to the dust;
>> revive me according to Your word. (v. 25)

> My soul weeps because of grief;
> strengthen me according to Your word. (v. 28)

> This is my comfort in my affliction,
> that Your word has revived me. (v. 50).

> If Your law had not been my delight,
> then I would have perished in my affliction. (v. 92)

> I am exceedingly afflicted;
> revive me, O Lord, according to Your word. (v. 107)

As pastors, we devote ourselves to the study of his Word, but sometimes we overlook the comfort of his Word. When confronted with turmoil and pain, we look for deliverance rather than perspective. While the Scriptures do not always promise us deliverance, they do bring clarity to the problems we face in life. Through the pages of Scripture, we find the answers that enable us to be spiritually revived even in the pain of ministry. It is when we discover this that we are truly equipped to proclaim God's message to a broken world.

However, even when we gain a better perspective of suffering, which enables us to see that there is a purpose in the events and circumstances of life, we still wrestle with our thoughts. But the biggest question is not the *what* or even the *why*, but the *who*.

4

Regaining a Perspective of God

How we perceive circumstances dictates how we respond to them. Imagine for a moment that you suffer a horrific accident caused by the negligence of a drunk driver. The accident results in your leg being crushed so badly that it forces the doctors to amputate the leg at the hip. You will no longer be able to go skiing. You no longer will be able to play games with your children or take long walks with your spouse. Every day becomes filled with the challenges of struggling with your handicap. Such an event would leave you bitter and angry, not just with the driver of the other car, but the circumstances confronting you. The foolish act of this other individual has unfairly caused you life-altering changes.

Now imagine a different set of circumstances. Your knee throbs severely, so you go to the doctor thinking you pinched a nerve or tore your MCL (medial collateral ligament). However, after a series of tests, the doctor confronts you with the tragic news that you have an aggressive form of bone cancer and you have a few short months to live. You go home, devastated by the news as you and your family prepare for the worst.

However, several days later, the doctor calls with some good news. After consulting specialists, they determined that if they removed the leg at the hip, not only would they be able to arrest the spread of the cancer, but also the prognosis would be a long and full life, albeit one faced with the struggles of having to live life with a handicap. Rather than being angry with the doctor for removing your leg, you rejoice and you go home with your family delighted that God used the skill of the doctor to bring you back from the grip of a certain death. The things you give up (skiing, playing sports, taking long walks with your spouse) seem minor compared to the joy of seeing your grandchildren.

In both scenarios, the events result in the same condition (life without the use of one leg). In one case we are left bitter and disappointed; in the other we are elated and thankful. What is the difference? Perspective. How we perceive an event dictates how we respond to the event.

But perspective is not the only mindset that profoundly influences our response to our experiences. Another is expectation. Unmet expectations lead to disappointment and bitterness. When we entered ministry we did so with a number of expectations of how people would treat us, what we would accomplish, and the benefits we would receive. But reality rarely matches dreams. People do not always treat us with respect and consideration. Ministry does not always go according to plan and we do not always enjoy the success we anticipated. We are continually told that strong leaders are clear visionaries. But what happens when your vision and plans for the future becomes your broken dreams? Proverbs 13:12 warns, "Hope deferred makes the heart sick, but desire fulfilled is a tree of life." When expectations are not met and dreams are shattered, you can easily become discouraged and disillusioned with ministry.

As rational beings, we filter every event through a theological grid. This grid dictates our understanding of the events happening in our life. Sometimes this grid is clearly understood and identified. Other times it dwells hidden in our subconscious, unrecognized, but dramatically influencing our perception of events and the expectations we have. This is especially true in our understanding of the difficulties and problems we face in ministry. Often we approach the struggles with a set of assumptions influencing how we understand and respond to the pain we face. Sometimes our theology and understanding of Scripture drive these assumptions. At other times, culture and our past shape our beliefs.

Because of our presuppositions, we often view suffering from strictly an emotional outlook, one where the emotional pain we experience controls our understanding of the circumstances we face. But suffering is not merely an emotional crisis; it is also a theological crisis. We can never discount the emotional impact that trials have upon our personal life. However, we must also follow the writers of Scripture whose theological understanding governed their emotional and spiritual reaction. To understand and properly respond to tribulations, we must not just look at how we view the events emotionally, but how we understand them theologically.

The book of Job is more than a book about personal suffering. It is a book that confronts our assumptions about God and about how he responds to the trials we experience. Just as Job and his three friends revealed many misguided beliefs, so also it is true that you and I have misguided and incorrect ideas about ministry and the struggles we face. But these assumptions deal with more than your assessment of suffering—they also deal with your viewpoint of ministry and how God works. At the center of the issue remains your understanding of how you discover the truth guiding your assumptions. Ultimately, Job and his friends did not struggle with just their understanding of pain and suffering, but how they understood truth and the basis for discovering truth.

ASSUMPTIONS ABOUT TRUTH AND SUFFERING

For Job and his friends, the debate was more than a dialogue about suffering and sin. The discussion was driven by the assumptions each had regarding how we determine the truth that dictates our understanding of God, of suffering, and of the experience of God's blessing. Each of them brought a different point of view to the table, but it was not until the end, when God entered the debate, that there came a radical change in their view of how they understood God and suffering.

Eliphaz: Understanding Suffering and
Blessing Based upon Personal Experience

The story of Job is familiar. Job, faced with the loss of all his possessions and everything important to him, expresses bitterness and bewilderment towards a silent heaven in search of an understanding of all that transpired in his life. When we read the book of Job, however, the extended speeches cause us our own bewilderment as we try to understand what role the three friends played in the story as both comforters and antagonists. However, when we look closer at the book, we discover that the problem with the three friends was not their lack of compassion and concern for Job. Anyone willing to sit on an ash heap for seven days and seven nights should not be judged as cold-hearted and uncaring (Job 2:13). The problem with the friends of Job was not their heart; it was their theology. In their desire to help Job, they felt compelled to correct Job and lead him back to repentance. While Job wrestled with the injustice of his suffering and a God who seemed distant and uncaring, his friends faced the problem of convincing Job of his sin and his need for repentance. Thus the debate raged back and forth in an argument where they may as well have been speaking different languages. As we are pulled into the dialogue through the beauty of Hebrew poetry, we soon begin to see that each of them had a different starting point in their assumptions.

After Job pours out his lament that not only reflected his emotional pain but also his deep crisis of faith, Eliphaz responded by reminding Job of all the times Job helped others going through adversity. However, Eliphaz then leveled his critique: Now that adversity has come upon him, Job responds with dismay and impatience. However, it is in chapter 4 that we see the underlying assumptions governing Eliphaz's viewpoint. Three times (4:8, 12; 5:3) in his first speech, Eliphaz appeals to personal experience as the basis for his understanding of suffering and Job's personal incident. In verse 8 he argues from experience, and his experience validates that those who sow trouble will harvest it. To support his premise, he appeals to nature by showing that even the fierce lion suffers because of his evil (4:8–11). He further appeals to his personal experience by describing a revelation he had, one that affirms that no one stands righteous before God. Then again in chapter 5, he states that he has seen the foolish take root but in the end they face only affliction (v. 3).

However, Eliphaz failed to recognize the inherent danger of developing a theology of God and suffering based upon experience. The grid of our own preconceived ideas filters our understanding of events in life. In other words, what we look for in our experience, will determine what we find. This results in our experience becoming a self-fulfilling prophecy. If we regard all suffering as a result of sin, then we will look for sin at the root of all causes; and, since we live in a sinful world, we will inevitably find some connection between the suffering we experience and the sin we have present in our own life or present in the lives of people around us. Since no one lives perfectly, and everyone, no matter how righteous, remains marred by sin, then the conclusion can be easily drawn that all suffering must be a result of either a failure on our own part or a failure on the part of others who we believe cause our suffering.

By appealing to experience, Eliphaz developed some assumptions that not only distorted his understanding of suffering, but of his understanding of God. Eliphaz looked at life and he saw that even the most righteous experienced the discipline of God because of sin. This we understand, for God demonstrates his love towards us by disciplining us (Prov. 3:11–12; cf. Heb. 12:4–5). Since no one is free from guilt, no one escapes the need of God's corrective hand. Furthermore, in his experience, Eliphaz observed that no one is righteous. Thus he concludes that since we suffer because of sin, and everyone is a sinner, therefore everyone who suffers must have sinned, and this causes us to face trials and difficulties (4:17). Consequently, the only proper response to affliction is repentance and confession (5:8). Even when Job protested his innocence, he fell right into the hands of Eliphaz's arguments. Rather than his protest causing Eliphaz to reconsider, it further confirmed Job's guilt, for no one can ever be guiltless. For Job to express anger and the injustice of God's discipline further confirmed to Eliphaz that Job endured hardship because of some deep rebellion (15:14–16).

Eliphaz's assumption, based on his own experience, not only affirmed that no one is righteous, but it also affirmed that only the wicked will suffer. Therefore, God will not cause the righteous to face affliction

(15:20). For Eliphaz, if we face adversity in our life, then it becomes de facto evidence that our relationship with God stands in peril (22:21–27).

Consequently, in his appeal to personal experience, he then shares how he himself would respond if he were in Job's position: he would seek God and place his cause before him (5:8). The same appeal undergirds the basis for his second speech in which he again declares what he has observed (15:17), namely, that the wicked always have difficulty in life. His conclusion: Job needs to repent of his sin before God will pour out his blessing again on Job's life (22:21–30).

While we readily condemn Eliphaz for his incorrect conclusion (for Scripture clearly does so), in reality we often fall prey to the same misguided conclusions. When we face struggles in ministry, we readily conclude that it must stem from some level of our sinfulness. Therefore, when adversity comes, it is always corrective at best (designed to correct some unknown character flaw) or punitive at worst (God bringing direct discipline because of a failure on our part).

As we read through the book of Job, it is not only important that we place ourselves in Job's position so that he becomes our voice in the midst of our suffering, but we must also see ourselves in Eliphaz. Certainly we can and should learn from every circumstance we face, good or bad. The problem arises when we start to make our experiences (or the experiences of others) normative for all people on all occasions. As was discussed earlier, one of the reasons that we struggle with dealing with trials and hardship in ministry is that those who have experienced blessings (usually in the form of numerical growth in the church) are then held up as the model to be normative for all pastors and church leaders. This gives us a false illusion that we should never experience difficulties and problems. Developing a theology of the church that is driven by experience distorts our perspective of God in two ways.

First, it leads us to a theology whereby God's blessing on our ministry is determined by our efforts rather than his grace and sovereignty. We assume that if we pray hard enough, work diligently enough, read the Bible religiously and sacrifice continually, we will experience the numerical growth that defines our understanding of God's blessing.

Conversely, if we face struggles and the church remains stagnant, then it is due to our lack of effort. But this ultimately undermines grace, for grace is giving us what we do not deserve—and never will deserve. Paul understood that any success in our ministry does not originate in our efforts but God's grace (2 Cor. 3:4–6).

Second, it leads us to a view of ministry where success is guaranteed by following certain principles. What has worked elsewhere should also work in every church. We pick up the latest issue of *Leadership Journal* or attend the latest conference, and those who have experienced success present their latest methods as the key for every church's success. Like Eliphaz, people further validate and legitimize their principles by claiming that God led them in implementing these principles. In the end, fads rather than Scripture drive our ministry. We look to the latest technique for answers to the lack of church growth. This is not to say that we cannot learn from what others have done. We can and we should. The problem arises when we make what others have done normative for all churches. This distorts God's work, for it can lead to an approach where God can be manipulated and governed by a set of rules normative in every circumstance. While God's character and will always govern his actions and he always acts consistent with his character, he does not act the same way in every situation. As we see in the book of Acts, he freed Paul and Peter from prison and the threat of death, while allowing Stephen to suffer martyrdom.

An experienced-based theology of ministry inevitably leads us down the wrong path where pragmatism becomes the driving force. If it works it must be right! This distorts our view of suffering. When you continue to experience frustration and discouragement and opposition, you begin to wonder if God has removed his blessing from your life. Since your experiences do not match the expectations constantly held up as the norm, it leads you to a personal and theological crisis. This distortion increases when you attend conferences where all you hear are testimonies of how God has blessed others' ministries through numerical growth. You hear of the number of baptisms people have had in the last year. You see how others have expanded their facilities and how programs transformed their church. It can appear that all the other churches seem to be having positive results and freedom from internal conflicts and problems, and you wonder why you and your church are so different. Why are we facing so many struggles when others seem to be so wonderfully blessed?

Bildad: Understanding Suffering Based upon Tradition

Whereas Eliphaz looks at life through his personal experience, Bildad takes it a step further by drawing upon the traditions that have been handed down through the generations. Bildad rightly recognized the limits of one's personal experience, so he appeals to the accumulative wisdom of previous generations (8:8). This tradition always trumps our own personal experience, for our knowledge is based on only a brief span of time while tradition has the value of generations of learning (vv. 9–10). However, for Bildad, because generations accumulated this wisdom, it becomes infallible; so the conclusions that they have drawn no longer remain open for question or possible exception. As a result, life and circumstances become a series of cause and effect where truth becomes black and white with no possible alternative. How God worked in the past provides certainty in terms of our understanding of how God will work in the present.

While he takes a different route than Eliphaz, he too comes to the same conclusion, namely, that Job's children died because of their sin (8:4). A just God always punishes the evildoer and blesses the righteous by prosperity and freedom from trials. Therefore, in order for Job to again experience blessing and prosperity, he must turn from his sin and return to his righteous living (vv. 5–7). Following the tradition of wisdom, Bildad appeals to the lessons of creation, appealing to the papyrus and spider, each pointing to the fragile nature of life and how there is no blessing apart from God.

This reliance upon tradition likewise distorts Bildad's understanding of God by leading Bildad to a number of false assumptions about how God works in the lives of people and how we are to understand the trials and difficulties we encounter. Bildad first assumes that God will always bring immediate relief to the crisis faced by the righteous (8:5–6). This takes our suffering to another level of understanding. In ministry we often understand that suffering will come, but what we do not understand—and what tormented Job—was the fact that in the face of our suffering heaven seems silent. When confronted with such silence, like Bildad, we assume that God will always swiftly act on behalf of those who live righteously. When God does not immediately bring deliverance, it must be because he is bringing some form of discipline or punishment on disobedience. Consequently, in our turmoil, we begin to doubt our standing before God. But this not only affects how we view ourselves, but also how we view others. When other pastors go through extended periods of turbulent circumstances, we easily become judgmental of them, assuming that the lack of deliverance must be because of some spiritual flaw in their life prohibiting God from acting on their behalf. We read books that constantly assure us that God will bless those who are godly, practicing all the spiritual disciplines (see 8:20–22). So we, like Bildad, conclude that the problems we face stem from our spiritual failures.

The end result is that we adapt the same theological framework governing Bildad; namely, we reap what we sow (18:8). If your spirituality directly causes all your trials in ministry, then you cause your own pain. But such thinking ultimately will undermine all ministry. If the suffering you experience always, directly or indirectly, relates to your own personal failure, you no longer have any hope. Instead of finding comfort and encouragement in the face of trials, you only find guilt and self-incrimination. Like Bildad, you are left with the conclusion that no one can find any encouragement in the midst of trials, because ultimately we can never gain acceptance before God (25:4–6). As a result, it should no longer surprise us that many pastors leave churches, broken, discouraged, and disillusioned with the very gospel they devoted their life to preach. While we proclaim a gospel of hope, we wrestle with the inward paradox that we ourselves have no hope.

However, the larger problem with tradition is that it can place blinders upon us so that we only see what we want to see. Such was the case for Bildad. Because of his adherence to tradition, anything that conflicted with the tradition was discounted as error. It also becomes a self-fulfilling prophecy. While tradition at times serves as an important guide, it is also a demanding mistress (to mix the metaphors). The danger of tradition is that it demands allegiance even above the Scrip ture. As we try to understand the various events that happen within the church, we often look to the knowledge of others. While this is helpful and important, it can also be misleading. We begin to assume that since God acted in the past in certain ways, then he should act in the present the same way. We guarantee our success merely by following a set of rules. If we pray the prayer of Jabez or try praying in circles, God will bless our life and ministry. If we practice principles followed by successful churches, positive things will always happen. Ministry becomes a formula rather than the mysterious work of God who accomplishes his purpose even when we cannot fully understand or perceive what that purpose is.

Traditions provide a basis by which we develop our expectations. Because tradition is based upon how events normally transpired in the past, we expect future events to follow the same pattern. When they fail to do so, it further adds to our confusion and frustration and the sense that somehow we have not been treated fairly. When you enter ministry, you develop a set of expectations of what you anticipate to achieve, how the ministry should go, and how you should be treated. You develop these expectations based upon the teaching of traditions. However, real life does not always play by the rules nor does it always follow the traditional model of ministry.

For example, in the past, people held the pastor in the community in high regard even if they did not attend church. But times have changed and this is no longer true. Instead of being warmly welcomed and respected, we receive a cold reception where people, not only in the community but in the church as well, see us an outsider to be viewed with suspicion. Consequently, we often feel isolated and alienated from even the community and the church. However, because we base our expectations upon past tradition, instead of recognizing the need for earning people's respect over time, we feel hurt and betrayed and begin to question whether or not we are cut out for the task. After all, if we are an effective pastor, tradition tells us that not only would we be immediately accepted, but we would have influence in the community. However, in the end this traditional view of ministry contradicts the teaching of Scripture where acceptance and respect by the world is the exception not the norm. Scripture warns that the norm will be ridicule, persecution, and rejection (John 15:18–19).

We find the same distorted expectations in our view of programs within the church. Traditionally, the Sunday school served as the backbone of the church, but many small churches today struggle to maintain a viable Sunday school program. Even when the church attracts young families, those families are not bringing their children to the Sunday school. So, here again, we struggle to identify what the problems might be. There must be something wrong with us since our Sunday school program flounders. It must be because we are failing to identify the right curriculum, no longer having a bus ministry, or failing to have enthusiastic teachers. You also see this in the current writings on the problem of the decline in the church in North America where the authors place the cause upon the pastors and congregations. If the church was more loving and the preaching more culturally relevant, then the church would grow. So we place more guilt upon the pastors and people. What we fail to recognize is that God still sovereignly governs the ministry of his church in the world. While we should always be focused upon the discipleship and training of children, it may be that traditional Sunday school is no longer the best approach. It may be that God is moving us in a different direction. Instead of thinking creatively, we, like Bildad, become blinded by our traditions and restricted by them.

Zophar: Understanding Suffering Based upon Wisdom

For Zophar, to answer the question of suffering one must not turn to either personal experience or tradition, but to the wisdom of the sages. Zophar exemplified the man of wisdom, the one who observed God's moral order established in creation (11:5–6, 20:4). Like the sage of Proverbs, Zophar upheld the ideals of wisdom and the capacity to discern truth. But he was not a mere intellectual who argued that man's reason could ultimately discover all truth. Instead, wisdom could come only from God, and man was ultimately responsible to learn wisdom from God (11:6). Because his sin blocked his ability to understand God's wisdom, Job could not find an answer to his suffering. However, his quest to uphold wisdom left Zophar as the cold and detached one. He saw life only from the sense of cause and effect, where failure to repent of one's sin stood at the source of all suffering. As a result, Zophar became rigid in his assumptions, namely, that the wicked can never have any blessing or joy in life (20:5–11) and a person's sin caused all his trials (20:12–19). While he may try to hide his rebellion, in the end it leads to his own self-destruction. For Zophar, sin blocks our ability to understand and observe God's ways. When we encounter heartaches without answers, then it stems from our sin.

However, Zophar fails to see the limits of wisdom—that we cannot fully understand or see all God does. While observation and wisdom give us understanding into some things about God, it does not give us a complete understanding. Traditional wisdom can distort our view of God by placing him in a straitjacket so he must act in the way that we think he should. We can conclude that God always brings judgment upon sin and that there is no hope for the fool to change (11:11–12). Consequently, we begin to view all blessings and sorrows directly related to our moral and inward righteousness. But this thinking does not allow for the exception, and it fails to recognize that while we can observe God's activity and purpose within nature, we cannot observe all that he does and why.

Wisdom literature was never meant to be absolutes for every situation; rather, it was general principles governing God's moral order. As literary expert Leland Ryken points out, "Unlike moral commands, proverbs tend to state general principles to which there might be exceptions. Those who utter proverbs do not worry about possible exceptions; they trust people to use their common sense in recognizing that a proverb need not cover every possible situation."[1] This generality within the nature of wisdom does not invalidate the truthfulness of the proverb, but it does allow for the possibility of the exception. The failure to recognize this possibility led Zophar to distort both his understanding of suffering and his understanding of God's activity.

Tragically in the church, we often take the same cold, calculated view of pastors facing hardships and difficulties. If you were doing a good job and following all the latest principles proclaimed in the current literature, then you would enjoy success. In the end, effectiveness in ministry can be orchestrated by adopting certain principles and programs. However, while God will never act inconsistent with his character, you cannot fully understand all his activities and how his character governs every event in your life. God often has purposes that are beyond the level of our understanding (Isa. 55:8–9; Rom. 11:33–36; 1 Cor. 13:12). This is what Zophar's reasoning failed to grasp. When we are going through suffering, we must recognize that we may not fully understand the *why*, but we can have unshakable trust in the *who*.

Job: When God Does Not Play by the Rules

Of all the participants within the story, it is with Job we most often identify with during times of trials. The problem of the three friends was that they not only had an incorrect understanding of suffering, but they had a distorted view of God himself, one where God only rewards the righteous and brings suffering upon the wicked. Instead of bringing comfort to Job and words of encouragement, they only served to add to his misery by failing to provide a clear and accurate view of God and his activity. Consequently, instead of condemning Job, they brought condemnation upon themselves by their words, for they misrepresented and distorted the very nature of God.

---

[1]   Leland Ryken, *How to Read the Bible as Literature . . . and Get More Out of It* (Grand Rapids: Zondervan, 1984), 124.

Likewise, when Job speaks, our initial response is to conclude that Job himself spoke rashly and sinfully. Yet, in the very beginning of the book, the author gave us a clue that this was not the case when he stated that Job "did not sin with his lips" (2:10). Thus he hints that in all of Job's harsh responses both to his friends and to God, Job remained righteous. The problem with Job was not sin, nor was it a wrong theology of God. Rather, the problem was an incomplete theology. Job couldn't understand when his daily experience did not match up to his understanding of God.

Of the four main participants (Job, Eliphaz, Bildad, and Zophar) only Job demonstrated a right perspective of God. What Job did not understand was how his understanding of God could be reconciled with the tragedies that he experienced. The bottom line for Job was that his catastrophes revealed an unfair God who was not playing by the rules. Job lived in a religious world where people could expect God to act a certain way. God, to be truly just, must act on his behalf and deliver him from any adversity and trial. When disaster first struck, Job remained firm in his trust that God would still take care of him (1:21–22). For Job, it was not a surprise that God would allow adversity and trials (2:10), but what he could not understand was the silence of heaven. If God brought us into the world only to suffer rather than experiencing his blessing, then what is the purpose of life (3:20–23)? This is what led to the paradox of faith. While Job could not reconcile his understanding of God with the suffering he was experiencing, he could not deny him or turn his back upon God (6:8–13).

Job concludes that never existing would have been better than a life of sorrow (3:11). Even Ecclesiastes, which agrees with the central theme of Job that traditional wisdom does not always provide adequate answers to the questions of life, argues that even with all the incongruities of life, it is still a gift from God to be enjoyed. But Job finds even that message to be a mockery. In the midst of his suffering, Job sees only the futility of life (7:1–2). The omnipresence of God becomes a curse rather than a blessing (vv. 19–21). As Job responds to the arguments of his friends, he reasons that if they are correct, then no one has any hope, since no one can be fully righteous before God (9:2). God becomes an unjust God who does not play by the very rules that he established for us to follow.

In the perplexity and paradox of Job's faith, we discover how our trials affect both our relationship with others and our relationship with God. First, our personal calamities lead to a feeling of isolation from even our closest allies (6:14). Even if our friends are not condemning us as Job's friends did, suffering still isolates us from them; even with all their sympathy, they do not fully understand our inward heartbreak. Second, and even worse, it leaves us with a feeling of isolation from God. In the midst of our pain, he seems indifferent and distant (9:13–18) where prayer seems empty and ineffective. Like Job, we can understand why we experience suffering, but what we cannot understand is why God remains hidden and indifferent to our need (23:3, 8–9) and to the wickedness that assaults us (24:12). We wrestle with the questions that suffering brings and why there seems to be no answer coming forth (13:21–24). It is one thing when Satan does not play by the rules, but it is quite another when it seems as if God does not either (21:7–9, 23–26).

This same perspective distorts our own view of frustrations and hurts in ministry. When we face problems we understand the reality of the suffering, but what we cannot understand is that heaven often seems silent. We wonder where is God's providential care. How can God be benevolent yet indifferent when we face personal attacks from antagonists who are not concerned about the ministry of Christ but their own position and power? Pastor and clinical psychologist Kenneth Haugk describes these individuals as people "who, on the basis of non-substantive evidence, go out of their way to make insatiable demands, usually attacking the person or performance of others. These attacks are selfish in nature, tearing down rather than building up, and are frequently directed against those in a leadership capacity."[2]

---

[2] Kenneth C. Haugk, *Antagonists in the Church: How to Identify and Deal with Destructive Conflict* (Minneapolis: Augsburg, 1988), 21–22.

When the church and even the board allows these individuals to attack the pastor and destroy his ministry in the church, we can at least chalk it up to the cowardice of sin-marred people plagued by their own inability to stand for truth. But what we cannot understand is why God does not quickly bring vindication. We begin to question God. Like Job, you begin to wonder if God called you to ministry, only to abandon you when you need him most. If ministry is a calling of God, then it becomes a curse rather than a blessing. You uphold the truth of Scripture and proclaim boldly the promises of God only to wonder inwardly why God does not seem to fulfill those very promises in your own life. If we faithfully proclaim that people must play by God's rules, then why does he not seem to play by the same rules in our own personal life?

Elihu: Are We Defending Ourselves or Defending God?

Elihu bursts onto the scene without any introduction. He is not present when the first friends arrive, and we do not know when he arrived at Job's ash heap. Unlike the other friends of Job, Elihu is neither condemned nor mentioned in the epilogue. But Elihu's presence is more than just an enigma. He serves to provide a bridge between the arguments of Job and his friends and the confrontation Job has with God. He sets the stage for God's appearance by moving the focus off of the suffering of Job over to the nature and activity of God. Unlike the three friends, and even Job, Elihu does not focus upon the *cause* of the suffering, but on our theology that guides our *response* to suffering. Elihu goes to the heart of the issue by pointing out the critical question: Are we focused on defending ourselves and vindicating our own character, or are we focused upon defending God and upholding his reputation and character (32:2–33; 33:12; 36:2)? Job wrestled with the apparent apathy of God and God's failure to take action in regards to both his circumstances as well as his questions. But Elihu points out that God is not accountable to us (33:13). When it seems to us as if God is not playing by the rules, it is not our position to question him. Rather, we must recognize that we must instead submit to him. God remains just in his actions even when our present experience appears to invalidate this (34:10–15).

Suffering shifts our focus. It moves your focus off of God and puts it on yourself and your circumstances. When going through the hardship of ministry, you easily lose sight of God. We become absorbed by the troubles confronting you and the circumstances disrupting your life and ministry. But Elihu calls us to shift the focus back upon God, his character, and his activity. Elihu reminds us that the purpose of life is not to attain comfort and prosperity but to glorify God in the midst of both our successes and tribulations. What brings glory to God is not our prosperity, but the affirmation of his justice and goodness in spite of the present burdens we face (35:6–7; 36:1–23).

We easily see God in the joys of life and that often is our focus. But is God's involvement in your life and ministry only found in the successes you experience? Is he absent when numbers decline, programs flounder, and buildings lack repair? Does conflict and pain always indicate the removal of his blessing? While Job's friend's argued that it does, Elihu reminds us that God remains present in the midst of the storm (36:24–37:24). Sometimes, God is most active when we cannot see any visible evidence of his work. Just as the storm, not just the clear day, reveals the power of God, so also the storms of life manifest the goodness and kindness of God (37:13).

When the pain overwhelms you, it is easy to become egocentric rather than theocentric. You become consumed by your own circumstances. You want deliverance from your pain. You want validation of your ministry. You want vindication from your distracters. You wrestle with the question, "Why am I experiencing these troubles?" But Elihu challenges us to remove the focus from ourselves, our reputation, our comfort, and our vindication and put it back upon God. God has not called us to a life of ease but a life of divine disclosure, where we reveal the character and nature of Christ through our attitudes and actions and even our agonies. We are not to seek our vindication before people. Instead, we are to seek to vindicate God through our submission to his will, even when that will takes us through the path of personal pain.

Throughout the whole book of Job, we read anxiously, waiting for the answer that Job and his friends (and we) so desperately sought. But the answer comes as a surprise. Instead of telling us why we experience so much grief and distress, God merely reminds us that he is God and that he never acts unfairly, capriciously, or unjustly. The problem was not with Job (as argued by his three friends), nor was the problem with God (as argued by Job), nor was it even their faulty view of suffering. Their problem was with their lack of understanding of God. Rather than God expounding upon the causes and reasons for suffering, he instead points us to himself and reminds us that he is God and we are not. That is all we need to know.

In chapters 38–39, God reminds Job (and us) that he is bigger than our understanding and beyond the realm of our total comprehension. To try to understand all of what God is doing and why he is doing it destines us to fail miserably. Instead, we must learn to trust him completely, even in the dark when we do not see him. We need to learn that he is mighty in power and he sustains all of creation (38:12–41). Furthermore, he remains intimately involved in all aspects of creation (chapter 39). The implication is obvious: If God is the one who creates and sustains all creation and he is intimately involved in all of creation, then he is the one who also creates, sustains, and remains intimately involved in our life as well.

But to see God's greatness, we must also see our smallness. In chapter 40–41, God forcefully reminds us that in his presence our smallness prohibits us from finding fault with him (40:2). Instead, we can only stand in humility before him (vv. 3–5), recognizing that he, not us, established the moral order governing the universe and our life (40:6–41:34). Consequently, in the midst of suffering we must not focus upon the circumstances, but focus upon the nature of God. We must trust that not only does he have the right to exercise his sovereignty, but he does so governed by his love and purpose. We must not trust God because we have all the answers. Rather, we must trust him in spite of the fact that we cannot attain the answers. We must trust him in the dark (42:2). Job did not receive the answers to his questions, nor did he receive any reason for his suffering. Even though the narrator gave us the answer to the mystery before the story unfolds, God never shared that information with Job. To trust God is not to understand all that God is and does. It is to come to the point where we trust him without any such understanding (vv. 5–6). What Job saw and heard and what he came to understand was not an explanation for his tragedies, but an unveiling of the reality of God in the midst of his personal pains.

There is one final chapter to the story that we cannot overlook, one that again is given to us so that we might have a more thorough understanding than even Job and his friends have. In the final chapter, we see the full restoration and vindication of Job as well as Job's offering of a sacrifice and intercession for his friends. However, we cannot escape the point that this restoration came at God's timing, not theirs (42:10–17). The New Testament gives us the full message. For the writers of the New Testament this final restoration and vindication for us will come in heaven when we receive the full rewards for our faithfulness and we gain his approval, not because of our effort, but because of his gracious and sovereign work in our life. When Paul speaks of the temporal tribulations we face, he reminds us that the purpose of our salvation is not found in our vindication in the present, but in the full restoration that comes in the age to come (2 Cor. 5:2–5). Like Job we wonder if relief will come and we will be restored. We wonder if we will ever experience God's vindication. The New Testament, and the book of Revelation in particular, give us the answer. Like Job we will receive the reward for our faithfulness, but it will come in God's timing, not ours. It comes not in the present, but in eternity.

Maintaining a Perspective of God in a Pleasure-Seeking Culture

While we affirm the central message of Job, we can fall prey to the same error that plagued Job and his friends. Because we live in a culture of pleasure, we view the pursuit of personal pleasure and happiness to be a personal right. We value personal happiness as the ultimate pursuit. In our pleasure-oriented culture, pain contradicts (at least in our minds) God's grace and sovereignty. How can God be sovereign and loving yet so indifferent to the pain we are experiencing? If I am going through difficult tribulations and misfortune, then something must be wrong. It is either that I am being punished for my shortcomings (Job's friends), or someone (including God) is violating my personal rights (Job). We fall into the very distortion that plagued Job and his friends, namely, that God is accountable to us and must play by our rules (or at least by the rules that we believe that he himself has established). If God does not act in the way we expect, we face the crisis between our experience and what we believe about God. This is further compounded by the fact that many of the struggles we face are caused by circumstances beyond our control.

Avoidance of Suffering

When we embrace the basic premise that suffering is always harmful, our focus shifts from ministry to the avoidance of suffering. We become afraid to stand for the truth if that stand will result in criticism, rejection, and personal pain. Our ministry becomes paralyzed as we shift from serving people to maintaining personal survival. As a result we become focused upon alleviating our own personal suffering, which distracts us from ministering to the needs of others. Even though we continue to fill the ministerial role, in many ways we have checked out. We may still be in the pulpit on Sunday but no longer engaged in the spiritual battle of confronting sin and transforming people. We start to do only the minimum, putting in our time but not our energy. We start to think, "What is the use?" Ministry requires a great deal of emotional and spiritual energy, and when trials come it saps our energy and leads to a sense of futility. Why should we put so much of our energy into something that seems pointless? Instead of allowing Scripture to set our agenda, we start to allow the congregation to set the agenda.

In commenting about the people's demand for a miracle in Numbers 11:10–13, pastor Blaine Allen writes, "When your ministry has become reduced to the quest for miracles, ask first one question: Who determined the need? Thirty-four hundred years ago, it was the flock. And God's Spirit at times does use the audience to *discern* needs, but not *define* them. The audience is not sovereign. Eugene H. Peterson stated, 'Sometimes I feel like a backwoods fundamentalists or somebody carrying a sign around Times Square that says REPENT. But I've been a pastor for thirty-five years, and I don't trust people one inch in defining what they need. We don't know ourselves.' Peterson continued, 'For me, being a pastor means being attentive to people. But the minute I start taking my cues from them, I quit being a pastor.'"[3] When you strive to please people rather than transform people, then you abandon your pastoral calling and become paralyzed in ministry (Gal. 1:9-10; 1 Cor. 4:1–5). You are not called to keep people happy and content, but to lead them in a radical transformation, conforming their thoughts and actions to the person of Christ (Col. 1:28–29). As a result, we no longer preach to transform people, we preach to appease them. Instead of telling them what they *need* to hear, we tell them only what they *want* to hear. We become social workers who minister only to felt needs rather than prophets who challenge people to abandon themselves to be conformed to the image of Christ.

---

[3] Blaine Allen, *Before You Quit: When Ministry Is Not What You Thought* (Grand Rapids: Kregel, 2001), 33. For Allen's quotation, see Eugene H. Peterson, "The Business of Making Saints," *Leadership Journal*, Spring 1997, 28.

Abandoning Ministry

The next step is the abandonment of ministry altogether. In 1 Kings 19 Elijah was ready to quit. When he challenged the prophets of Baal to a contest, he was not only confident that God would act, but that the people of Israel would respond to the display with a massive turning away from idolatry and back to the worship of God. With this goal in mind, he stacked the rocks one upon another and then poured water upon the altar in order to show conclusively that Yahweh was God. But tragically, instead of the people responding with repentance, they gave a collective yawn of indifference. Then, to top it all off, instead of the people rallying around him, he faced the vengeance of a pagan queen obsessed on his personal and professional destruction. What he felt would be a decisive victory for God had all the earmarks of a colossal failure. Discouraged and disillusioned, he ran into the wilderness, ready to quit ministry and even life itself.

When the church struggles and opposition arises, we often become dispirited and cynical to the point that we begin to wonder if we are genuinely called. Like Elijah, we have expectations that our ministry will change lives, and that people will respond to our message. While you recognize that you will not always please everyone, you are never prepared for the personal attacks directed at you. Even though you do not expect everyone to be radically transformed by your preaching, you do expect some to be. When it does not happen, you begin to question your abilities and calling. Instead of confidence in what God can do through us, we become plagued by self-doubt and insecurities that drive us out of ministry.

Seeds of Doubt and Distortion

But even worse, the struggles we face not only lead to doubts about our own capabilities, it leads to a distortion of our understanding of God. Like Job, we begin to wonder if God is who he says he is. Instead of

God being a loving God who provides for all our needs, he becomes a capricious God who seems to act without reason. We often struggle to understand why God seems to be blessing others, even those who seem to be compromising the message of Scripture, yet bestows no blessing upon our ministry even though we are seeking to walk in obedience to him. We feel the constant pressure to have our church growing numerically but often become discouraged when no matter how we work, the numbers remain stagnant and heaven remains silent.

Conferences and books constantly tell us that if we pray hard enough and work diligently enough numerical growth will happen. Books fill the Christian bookstores proclaiming that if you say this prayer or institute this program or follow these principles, God's blessing will be poured out upon your life. But reality does not often match expectations, and the result is that we, like Job and Elijah, become disillusioned with God and begin to question what we believe about him. We become angry with God, feeling that he has abandoned and forsaken us at worse, or overlooked and ignored our ministry at best.

When our present experience does not match the hopes we have, then we begin to question everything about our ministry. We see churches that have compromised the message of Scripture continue to increase and enjoy popularity and we begin to compromise ourselves in order to gain the popularity we so often see. When the alleviation of suffering becomes our primary objection, we will inevitably start to say only what people want to hear. However, it does not stop there. It leads us to begin to question the Bible itself. We stop believing the Bible has all the answers because we fail to have the answers to the pain that we ourselves experience. If the Bible is not sufficient for us, how can it be sufficient for the people that we serve? It is no wonder that many of the sermons preached from pulpits today proclaim more pop psychology than theological truth. The message of the church in such cases has little to distinguish it from the self-help gurus populating secular airways. The message of Scripture that calls for radical transformation becomes a message of self-actualization.

Sour Grapes

But perhaps the greatest effect that our perception or misconceptions have is upon our attitude toward the very people we serve. Instead of seeing others within the church as co-workers and fellow heirs, we develop an "us-versus-them" mentality. We become cynical and see anyone who disagrees with us as antagonists, driven by selfish desires. Tragically, many pastors have become bitter towards the very people that they are called to love. One pastor of a larger church went so far as to say that a church will only grow when led by the paid staff rather than volunteer elders or deacons. For him, the only way a church could truly be effective is if the congregation gives full authority and power within the church to the pastor. While there are certainly churches where the lay leaders within the church are antagonists who want nothing more than power and control, usually this is not the case. Somewhere along the line the pastor suffered personal attacks making him bitter and distrusting of the people he served. Tragically, this is played out too often and the result is that the ministry becomes hamstrung by suspicion and mistrust rather than mutual respect.

Bargaining with God

All this leads to bargaining with God to try to earn his blessings and alleviate our trial. Like Job and his friends, we ultimately believe that success can be earned through our acts of righteousness. If we are going through trouble and trials in ministry, then it must be a result of either our sin or the sin of the people. We constantly live with guilt that we are not doing enough or being spiritual enough. So we begin to barter with God. If he will bless our ministry, then we will do more for him.

However, this contradicts the very nature of grace. The Scripture boldly proclaims that no matter what we do, how hard we try, or how righteous we live, we remain marred by sin so that God's blessing can never be attained by our efforts. Paul understood this when he wrote, "For I am the least of the apostles, and not fit to be called an apostle, because I persecuted the church of God. But by the grace of God I am what I am, and His grace toward me did not prove vain; but I labored even more than all of them, yet not I, but the grace of God with me" (1 Cor. 15:7–10). Whatever we experience in ministry is a work of God's grace rather than a result of our own efforts. Too often we as preachers proclaim the undeserving grace of God, but in our daily practice still seek to earn God's blessing upon our ministry.

Letting God Be God Even in Our Suffering

But this is what leads us to the same question perplexing Job and his friends. The real question that Job and his friends needed to answer did not deal with the cause of suffering but their perspective of God in the midst of suffering. More often than not, when experiencing discouragement and frustration in ministry, our focus shifts to the cause, and how to alleviate or deal with it, rather than looking at our understanding of God. Elihu, who sets the stage for God's response to Job, rightly pointed out that God's grace remains untouched by our sin and by our righteousness: "If you have sinned, what do you accomplish against him? And if your transgressions are many, what do you do to Him? If you are righteous, what do you give to Him, or what does He receive from your hand? Your wickedness is for a man like yourself, and your righteousness is for a son of man" (Job 35:6–8). In ministry, we must allow God to be God and to do as he pleases with us and through us because his work is not dependent upon us. His grace is such that he can use us in spite of our failures, and he will sovereignly accomplish his purpose without any need of us (Acts 17:25). He is sufficient in himself. While this is not a license to sin, it is a reminder that we cannot earn his blessings, nor do we have anything intrinsic within ourselves that guarantees our own personal success.

At the risk of sounding harsh what we must always remember is that *he is God and we are not—deal with it!* He has the right to take us through whatever experience and hardship he desires if that brings him the most glory. We must ground our view of life and pain in this truth.

The way to deal with frustration and discouragement in ministry is not to change our circumstances to alleviate our pain, but to change our view of God that distorts our response to the problems we face.

As we face the struggles of ministry, we must first affirm the good ness and sovereignty of God. We must affirm that regardless of our circumstances these truths remain an unchangeable constant. As parents, we try to answer all our children's questions when we tell them to do something. But often they continue to press with the ultimate question, "Why?" There finally comes a point when we realize that no matter how much reasoning we give, the question will never be answered. Finally we reach the point when we answer, "Because; that's why!" There comes a time when a child must simply trust our wisdom as parents because we are the parent.

This is what God reminds us in Job. For all his patience in allowing us to ask "why," there comes a time when we need to just accept that God is God. We may not know why, but we can learn to trust him even with the questions. Paul reminds us of this in Romans 8. In a chapter that highlights the tribulation we experience because we live in a fallen world, he concludes with one of the greatest affirmations of God's constant love found in all of Scripture. We can remain confidence and at peace even as we struggle with the questions because we know that we have a God whose love remains both constant and unchallenged by any circumstance or situation we face in life.

Second, we must affirm God's purpose for our life and ministry. His purpose is not to make us feel good, but to make us good. We are not called to a life of pleasure and comfort. We are called to proclaim Christ, a calling where he must increase and we must decrease. Because he is infinitely wiser than us, we must trust in his purpose. When confronted with trials, we easily start to doubt his purpose. How can his purpose be best when it encompasses so much pain? But God has an eternal purpose in all that he does, and it is for our ultimate good even if we cannot see that good at the moment of our trial. Consequently, we will affirm with Paul: "We know that God causes all things to work together for good to those who love God, to those who are called according to his purpose" (Rom. 8:28). Then, to support and affirm the sanctifying purpose of God in our life, he provides the basis for our confidence in verses 29–30: "For [in a causal sense] those whom He foreknew, He also predestined to become conformed to the image of His Son, so that He would be the firstborn among many brethren; and these whom He predestined, He also called; and these whom He called, He also justified; and these whom He justified, He also glorified." While you may not understand how the present circumstances fit into God's purpose, he has already revealed to us what his purpose is—our glorification.

Affirming these things about God gives us new perspective, yet even as we gain an understanding of who God is, we are left with another question, a question that goes to the very core of our identity as we walk upon our journey. The journey we travel is not just about who God is, but it is also about who we are and who we are becoming.

5

Regaining a Perspective of Ourselves

RECOGNIZING OUR POSITION AND PURPOSE

To understand why so many pastors leave the ministry, it is necessary for us to do more than merely identify ways that we distort our view of ministry. The problem goes far deeper than that, for it goes to the heart of our understanding of God and his activity within our life. As pastors, elders, and other ministry leaders we often affirm that the circumstances surrounding us should not drive our attitudes and actions in life. Instead, we challenge people to learn to be content in all circumstances (Phil. 4:11–10). However, our personal reality does not often match the message we proclaim. Within our own life and ministry, we often fail to recognize that circumstances do not cause the stress we feel. We fail to realize that the stress we experience stems from our own personal attitudes rather than the situations themselves. Too often we blame others for the inward tensions we experience in ministry, believing that if our congregation would only respond differently, then our ministry would be more enjoyable. So we leave the church and go to another in search of greener pastures only to find the same problems following us to the new field. While the names and faces of the people and the specifics of the problems and trials we face change, the pressures and stresses do not. The challenge is not to change our situation, but to change our understanding of God, our ministry, and ourselves.

As we read the pages of Scripture, we discover that the early church leaders not only faced the same problems and difficulties we confront today, but in many ways they dealt with challenges that would cause the most dedicated pastor to question and abandon his calling. They faced the problems of public criticism (1 Cor. 4:3–5). They coped with the dilemma of bringing unity to churches torn apart by a cult following of specific individuals (3:4). They confronted divisions and bickering between individuals within the congregation (Phil. 4:2). They needed to bring spiritual healing and guidance to immature churches (Heb. 5:12). They had to deal with churches who became enamored with teachers who filled their heart and mind with false doctrine (Gal. 1:6). They struggled to respond to people critical of their preaching and leadership (2 Cor. 10:1, 10). If the internal pressures of dealing with the church were not enough, they faced the continual threat of death by the Jews and Romans who sought to silence their message. Paul well understood both the internal and external cost of ministry when he summarizes the realities of his own ministry:

> Are they servants of Christ?—I speak as if insane—I more so; in far more labors, in far more imprisonments, beaten times without number, often in danger of death. Five times I received from the Jews thirty-nine lashes. Three times I was beaten with rods, once I was stoned, three times I was shipwrecked, a night and a day I have spent in the deep. I have been on frequent journeys, in dangers from rivers, dangers from robbers, dangers from my countrymen, dangers from the Gentiles, dangers in the city, dangers in the wilderness, dangers on the sea, dangers among false brethren; I have been in labor and hardship, through many sleepless nights, in hunger and thirst, often without food, in cold and exposure. Apart from such external things, there is the daily pressure on me of concern for all the churches. Who is weak without my being weak? Who is led into sin without my intense concern? (2 Cor. 11:23–29)

Where Paul persevered, many of us (myself included) would have long ago quit. The call to serve people is one thing; the reality of being in a physical, emotional, and spiritual meat grinder is a whole different story. However, rather than shrink back and look for a different line of work, Paul rejoiced in his suffering on behalf of the church (Col. 1:24).

What was the difference? Why was it that the early church leaders prospered in adversity while we often turn tail and run? Why did Paul consider It a mark of God's activity in his life that he remained faithful in ministry, not succumbing to the pressures (1 Tim. 1:12)? Even after such severe trials, why was Paul able to say with such confidence that he fought the good fight and finished the race when so many of us abandon the race (2 Tim. 4:6–8)?

It was not because his ministry was easier than ours, for he himself stated that he was poured out as a drink offering. At the end of his life, Paul considered himself to be used up and burned up, a sacrifice ready to be placed on the altar, a life of service only to be completed by his death. Paul was not stating mere platitudes when he encouraged Timothy to "endure hardship" (2 Tim. 4:5). He spoke from first-hand experience. If I had to endure all the hardships of Paul, would I have finished the race, or quickly abandoned it to go in search of the box seats where I could enjoy all the luxuries of an observer? I have my doubts. Certainly in my own strength I would have quickly joined the fans in the stands. What was different about Paul, the other apostles, and their associates? Why did they remain in the race at such a personal cost? The answer lies no further than their perspective about themselves and what it meant to be called into ministry.

SLAVES OF CHRIST: THE ATTITUDE OF A LEADER

In our modern approach to ministry, we view ourselves as leaders of organizations. Like a president or owner of a company, we assume the people we serve will regard us with a certain amount of respect and honor. When it does not happen, we feel disrespected and devalued. When people criticize us or respond with negative comments to the ideas and programs we seek to implement, we feel a certain amount of personal offense. After all, have we not spent years in preparation for the ministry, and are we not the "experts" of the ministry of the church? No one questions the engineer or the scientist when they speak authoritatively, yet people continue to question our decisions and our understanding of Scripture.

Readjusting Our Perspective

This personal and professional rejection was not unknown to the disciples. Even though Paul was one of the greatest theologians of church history, he faced continual attacks and criticisms by people in the church of Corinth. However, rather than allow them to cause him to become bitter or discouraged, he continued to effectively serve them even though they were highly critical of him. While Paul would answer his critics, he did not allow them to either become a distraction (1 Cor. 4:3–4) or a hindrance. Instead, he sought to continue to love and minister to the very people most critical of him (2 Cor. 11:1).

When we look into the pages of Scripture, we discover that the call to be a prophet and preacher of Christ resulted in severe persecution and suffering (Heb. 11). Yet in the midst of their struggles, like their Old Testament counterparts early Christian leaders not only maintained their commitment to proclaim Christ, but often rejoiced in the midst of their suffering. Where we would have long ago abandoned the ministry in pursuit of a more comfortable career, they stood firm. But when we closely examine their lives, we discover that they were not supersaints immune to the discouragements we struggle with so much. Paul experienced the same temptations of sin we face (Rom. 7:18–24). He struggled at times with discouragement, inward anxieties, and fears (2 Cor. 7:5; 11: 28–29). Yet in the midst of all their trials, he did not lose heart but instead remained faithful (4:1, 16). What was the difference? Why did Paul and the prophets remain in the ministry whereas so many today leave disillusioned and discouraged?

The answer to that question lies in their perspective. They did not see themselves as leaders and executives given a position of honor and respect within the church. When we look at the metaphors and terms they used to describe themselves, we discover a different outlook. Perhaps the greatest cause of pastors and other church leaders abandoning ministry today is not the treatment they receive from others, but their view of their ministry and themselves that leads to faulty expectations of how others, and even God, should treat them.

The Perspective of a Slave

While we often see ourselves as leaders and the head of an organization, the apostles saw themselves as slaves of Christ. Throughout the New Testament the concept of slavery served to define the apostles' understanding of themselves and their relationship to the church (Rom. 1:1; Phil. 1:1; 2 Peter 1:1; Rev. 19:5; Gal. 1:10). What distinguished the apostles from the rest of us was not their innate abilities or circumstances, but their grasp of who they were and what they were called to be.

Romanian pastor Josef Tson, who had been imprisoned for his faith under the Communist Ceaușescu regime and was later exiled, captured this difference when he expressed his preference to be introduced simply as "a slave of Jesus Christ." Tson forcefully expressed his preference at a conference: "'There aren't many people,' he observed, 'who are willing to introduce me as a slave. They substitute the word 'servant' for 'slave.' In twentieth-century Christianity we have replaced the expression 'total surrender' with the word 'commitment,' and 'slave' with 'servant.' But there is an important difference. A servant gives service to someone, but a slave belongs to someone. We commit ourselves to do something, but when we surrender ourselves to someone, we give ourselves up."[1] For his disciples, that which defined their identity and their position in relationship to Christ and in relationship to the ministry was the fact that they were slaves of Christ.

The fact that the writers of the New Testament would use the term "slave" was shocking and filled with implications to the readers. The writers of Scripture used metaphors, not because they were picturesque, but because they captured the essence of what the apostles were trying

---

[1]   Quoted in Murray J. Harris, *Slave of Christ: A New Testament Metaphor for Total Devotion to Christ* (Downers Grove, IL: InterVarsity Press, 1999), 18.

to teach. For them to use the metaphor of a slave was both graphic and real, for the concept of slavery was not remote as it is today. Nor was it sanitized by the concept of a servant that is often used in translations today. As MacArthur points out, "While it is true that the duties of slave and servant may overlap to some degree, there is a key distinction between the two: servants are hired; slaves are owned. Servants have an element of freedom in choosing whom they work for and what they do. The idea of servanthood maintains some level of self-autonomy and personal rights. Slaves, on the other hand, had no freedom, autonomy, or rights."[2] The striking metaphor vividly pointed to the attitude and position that governed the apostles' worldview.

MacArthur notes further that in the New Testament, "a slave (whether literal or figurative) was someone whose person and service belong wholly to another. On this view slavery involves (a) absolute ownership and control on the part of the master and total subjection of the slave, and (b) the absence of the slave's freedom to choose his action or movement."[3] To regard oneself as a slave was to recognize that one's life was no longer his or her own, but belonged solely to the authority and dictates of the master. Gaius, the Roman jurist during this period, described the legal position of a slave in his *Institutes*: "Slaves are in the power of their masters, and this power is acknowledged by the ius gentium [Law of Nations], for we know that among all nations alike the master has the power of life and death over his slaves, and whatever property is acquired by a slave is acquired by his master."[4] When Paul and the other writers of the New Testament referred to themselves as slaves of Christ, they acknowledged that they abandoned the freedom

---

[2] John MacArthur, *Slave: The Hidden Truth about Your Identity in Christ* (Nashville: Thomas Nelson, 2010), 17.

[3] Ibid., 26.

[4] Text of this quotation and its translation by S. P. Scott based on Gaius, *The Institutes of Gaius*, ed. Francis De Zulueta, 2 pts. (Oxford: Clarendon Press, 1946–53), pt. 1, bk. 1, §52, accessed October 23, 2013, http://faculty.cua.edu/pennington/law508/roman%20law/GaiusInstitutesEnglish.htm.

to choose their actions and movements. Instead, they affirmed that they could only do what the master desired.[5]

We often approach ministry in the church as an occupation where our participation is voluntary. Because we freely give of ourselves for others, we expect some appreciation and respect in return. When circumstances get difficult and costly, we believe we possess the right to leave the ministry to pursue more comfortable and lucrative pursuits. We easily become more captives of our culture than of Christ. But as a slave, Paul possessed no such right and freedom. The will of his master completely governed his life, constraining him to preach and minister the gospel no matter how difficult or costly the ministry became to him personally (1 Cor. 9:16). For Paul, the call to ministry was not a voluntary call, but one born in his understanding of his relationship with God and his redemption. Similarly, we did not choose to be pastors; it was a calling and task chosen for us by the sovereign God.

Within the Roman culture, there were two primary ways that a person became a slave. The first was to be captured in war and become a prisoner who then became a slave to the conquering army. After his capture, the victors forced him to take the yoke of slavery upon himself, symbolized by passing underneath three spears lashed together to form a doorway. This was referred to as passing "under the yoke" (1 Tim. 6:1).[6] This became synonymous to Christian conversion, which may be described as an exchange of yokes. Our new obligation and service to Christ replaced our old obligation to sin.[7] Paul's statement that he was a prisoner "for" Christ may also be translated "a prisoner 'of' Christ" (the genitive of possession rather than purpose) (Eph. 3:1; 4:1). Thus the verse serves as a play on both words and circumstances, "that in being a prisoner for Christ and to being a prisoner, that is a slave of Christ."[8]

---

[5]   Harris, *Slave of Christ*, 26.

[6]   Francis Lyall, *Slaves, Citizens, Sons: Legal Metaphors in the Epistles* (Grand Rapids: Zondervan, 1984), 31.

[7]   Harris, *Slave of Christ*, 94.

[8]   Lyall, *Slaves, Citizens, Sons*, 30.

Second, a person became a slave when someone purchased them in the marketplace. This may come about because a person sold himself or herself into slavery to pay a debt or was sold into slavery by another to pay a debt. In any case, the one who purchased the slave become the legal owner of the individual. Paul again saw his relationship with Christ in terms of this legal transaction (Rom. 6:16–22). Because Christ purchased him, he was no longer a freeman, but one who was sold as a slave to Christ so that Christ had absolute authority over his life and conduct (1 Cor. 6:20). Because of this, rather than being governed by others, Paul was only governed by God (1 Cor. 7:23; Eph. 6:6; Gal. 1:10).

Living in Submission to the Master

This understanding of their servitude to God transformed the early Christian leaders' view of themselves and their involvement in ministry. The same is equally true of us today. As a slave, we no longer live for our own pursuits and desires. Instead, our sole desire is to please and do the will of the master (Rom. 6:16; Luke 17:10). This means that we recognize God's right to exert absolute dominion over us as our master. Consequently, we make every effort to do the master's will to the full extent of our abilities.

We are to be wholly committed to serve our master's interest and not our own.[9] As New Testament scholar Murray J. Harris points out, "The essence of slavery is subjection, usually involuntary, to the will of another. . . . The slave is totally at the disposal of his master, completely subject to his master's will. He lives solely for the benefit of his master, and the service he must render has two elements: obedience to explicit commands, and, where there are no specific directives to follow, actions that will please his master."[10] He goes on to state, "In a fundamental sense slavery involve the absence of rights, especially the right to determine the course of one's life and use of one's energies. What is

---

[9]   Ibid., 30.

[10]   Harris, *Slave of Christ*, 95.

denied the slave is freedom of action and freedom of movement; he cannot do what he wishes or go where he wishes. The faculty of free choice and the power of refusal are denied him."[11] The point then is that as ministers we are no longer free to enter and leave ministry as if it was a profession bestowed upon us as an option. Rather, it is a calling of the master that is governed by the will of the master. We can only leave the ministry if Christ determines that we can serve him better in another venue. This shifts our focus from our own success and pleasure to the sole purpose of accomplishing Christ's will.

But this also means that we can expect no better treatment than the treatment the master himself receives. If people hate our master, they will equally hate us. If they mistreat the master, then they will mistreat us (John 15:18–20). We can expect no less than what the master experienced. Since Christ's servitude to the Father resulted in suffering (Phil. 2:7–9), then we must equally recognize that in the service of Christ we will also experience suffering and hardship (1 Peter 2:18–20).[12] We often feel angry when we encounter difficulties, criticisms, and personal attacks in ministry, believing that we are worthy of more respect than we are receiving. But if the master experienced these trials, then we should not be surprised when we encounter the same opposition.

But the implications of our slavery also strike at the very core of our attitude and relationship to the congregation. In ministry, we can leave the church bitter and angry because the church failed to adequately care for our physical and emotional needs. We become frustrated because the church seems indifferent to our financial pressures. We become angry when people criticize us for even a minor "luxury," stating, "We must be paying the pastor too much because I can't afford that." While we do not expect an exuberant pay, it would be nice not to face the monthly pressures of making ends meet. This resentment grows when we start to approach our retirement and realize we have nothing except

---

[11] Ibid., 107.

[12] Ibid.

Social Security to rely upon. It is no wonder that financial concerns and worries remain one of the main pressures that pastor's face.

However, the problem is not with the church and the attitude of the congregation in providing for the pastor. The problem lies with us and our misguided expectation that the church is responsible for our well-being. Intrinsic in the concept of a slave is the fact that the slave is completely and solely dependent upon the master for his care and provision. Christ takes this responsibility solely upon himself. While he may use the congregation and the church to provide for our needs, he is not limited by the church. He may choose a completely different avenue to provide for us. When we become bitter towards the congregation because they "did not care for us," we place an illegitimate expectation upon the church. God is the source of our provision. Paul recognized this when encouraging the church to give to his needs. He did not look to them for his needs, nor demand that they give to him (2 Cor. 11:7–11). Instead, he was trusted in the provision of his master (Phil. 4:10–14).

For Paul and the apostles, as servants of Christ and under his dominion, God possessed the right to allow them to suffer if it ultimately accomplished his purpose. Because of this, they did not see their pressures and trials as something to drive them from ministry. Rather, they embraced them gladly recognizing that part of the privilege of being a slave of Christ and part of God's activity in accomplishing his purpose through them involved personal pain (Phil. 3:10). When you accept Christ and accept his call, you accept his absolute authority over your life and your ministry. He has the freedom and right to take you through whatever circumstances you may face in order to accomplish his will. Like Job, in our quest to understand why we face struggles, we must learn to live with the tension of not knowing the answers to the *why*. Instead, we must remember that God is God and he is our master and he has the right to do as he pleases in our life.

But this does not lead us to fatalism, being at the mercy of the whims of a capricious God who arbitrarily does whatever he desires. In the slave-master relationship, the nature, position, and character of the master determined the condition and status of the slave. In many cases, if the owner was highly regarded in the society, the slave would attain a position of honor in the community exceeding even a free-man.[13] Because of his status and relationship to the master, a slave may choose to remain as a slave rather than obtain his freedom (Exod. 21:6).[14] It is because of the character of our master that we can trust him completely.

Christ is the perfect master; our service for him is not done under compulsion and fear of punishment for disobedience, but voluntarily, with the desire to please him.[15] His yoke is easy and his burden is light (Matt. 11:30). Therefore, while he may allow us to experience suffering, it ultimately pales in comparison to the reward he gives. He never allows his slave to experience arbitrary trials without eternal reason. God does not bring suffering merely for suffering's sake. It always has a purpose and a reason even though we may not understand what that reason will be. Even though we may not understand why we experience the trials, we can rest in the fact that we have a benevolent master who ultimately has his eternal purpose and our best interests (and those two are never in conflict) at the forefront of his activities in our life.

Serving as Slaves to the Church

Paul then takes his view of slavery one step further when he surprisingly states that not only was he a slave to Christ, but he also saw himself as a slave to the church (2 Cor. 4:5). At first glance, this seems to be a contradiction to his relationship to Christ, for how can one have two masters? Paul makes it clear that this does not mean that we are slaves to people's whims and demands within the church. This would contradict what Paul already stated in 1 Corinthians 7:23: "You were bought with a price; do not become slaves of men." When Christ purchased us from slavery to sin, he also freed us from enslavement to the opinions

---

13   Ibid., 135.

14   Ibid., 36.

15   Ibid., 97.

and legalistic demands of others. He further clarifies this in 1 Corinthians 4:3–4. To become enslaved to the opinions of others is to no longer be a slave to Christ.

Yet, in 1 Corinthians 9:19, Paul states that he willingly became a slave to others in order to win more people for Christ. By this he followed Christ's example for Christ himself willingly set aside his divine rights and became a slave in order to redeem humanity (Phil. 2:7). Even though Christ was the Son of God, as author John Bevere notes, "He did not come to be served but to serve. He was the Son. He was free. He owed no one anything. He was subject to no man. Yet He chose to use His liberty and freedom to serve."[16] Likewise, Paul expressed his slavery to Christ (and freedom in Christ) by willingly setting aside the exercise of his rights and privileges as a slave (and the high honor and freedom that came because of it) in order to willingly serving people for their spiritual growth.

Concerning 2 Corinthians 4:1–6, Harris points out:

> It is tempting (and certainly grammatically possible) to regard the conjunction *de* here as meaning "and therefore," and not simply "and": "It is not ourselves that we present, but Jesus Christ as Lord, *and therefore* ourselves as your slaves." This parallelism and the natural sequence of thought from lordship to slavery suggests that acknowledgement of the lordship of Jesus leads naturally and inevitably to lowly, unquestioned service to one's fellow-believers. To confess "Jesus is Lord" is to say to other followers of Jesus, "I am your slave." Slavery to Christ is exhibited in slavery to Christians. Because of their willing servitude to Christ, and as part of it, Christians are unconditionally obligated to serve Christ's people.[17]

By focusing on his enslavement to Christ, Paul radically reorients our reference away from seeing the church as a means for our success

---

[16] John Bevere, *The Bait of Satan*, rev. ed. (Lake Mary, FL: Charisma House, 2004), 113.

[17] Harris, *Slave of Christ*, 103.

and seeing people as a tool to be used. Paul, being a slave to the church, did not contradict his servitude to Christ, it served to be the means by which he expressed Christ's ownership of him. By willingly becoming a slave to the church Paul revealed his obedience to Christ

Christ points to this realignment of our understanding of leadership when he confronts the disciples about their desire to be the greatest in the kingdom. When two of the disciples (James and John) requested to be granted the highest positions of prominence in the kingdom of Christ, the rest of the disciples became angry (Mark 10:35–52) for they too wanted to be in the place of preeminence. In order to correct them Christ calls them together and tells them, "You know that those who are recognized as rulers of the Gentiles lord [i.e., to rule to one's advantage] it over them; and their great men exercise authority [literally, to play the tyrant] over them. But it is not this way among you, but whoever wishes to become great among you shall be your servant; and whoever wishes to be first among you shall be slave of all" (vv. 42–44). In this rebuke he informs them that the concept of leadership in his kingdom is fundamentally different from the world. The world views leadership from the standpoint of power and authority where leaders use people to achieve their own ends. But the kingdom principle of leadership is that a leader is a slave to the rest.

While we often make a logical break between verses 45 and 46 and thus see them as unrelated events, the text draws the two events together. It is important to see that discussion of the nature of leadership and the healing of the Bartimaeus are grammatically linked together. The identical question asked in verse 36 and again in verse 51 serve to provide a grammatical and logical bracket linking the two events into one story with the healing of Bartimaeus serving as an illustration of what servant leadership means. Servant leadership is not getting others to do what benefits us (as in secular leadership); rather, it is seeking to do what benefits them (as in the case of Christ healing Bartimaeus). Too often pastors and other church leaders see the congregation as tools to use to insure their success rather than setting aside their own reputation and success in order to assist the growth and ministry of others. It is the secular pyramid of leadership turned upside down. The congregation does not exist to serve us and our vision; rather, we exist to serve them in the pursuit of their ministry (see also Eph. 4:11–12).

SHEPHERDS OF CHRIST: THE FUNCTION OF A LEADER

While the metaphor of a slave highlights the attitude we are to have, it is the image of a shepherd that serves to highlight the function and nature of a leader in both the Old and New Testaments. In our modern reading of the text, we often develop an idealistic view of shepherds. When we use the term, we often think of a tranquil pastoral setting in which the shepherd enjoys the day sitting on a rock with the warmth of the sun beating down as he watches the sheep frolic in the grass. But reality is far different. Growing up on the farm and working with livestock, I quickly learned that caring for animals requires hard and often painful work. I remember going out with my father in the worst weather to care for the animals, often getting up at all hours of the night to tend to a sick, smelly cow that was more than willing to give a well-timed kick to reward you for your efforts.

Being a shepherd is not a calling for the timid and weak. It involves basing your whole life and schedule around the needs and care of the sheep. The ones whom you are trying to help the most sometimes are the very ones who turn against you. Sick animals needing care and attention are at times the most cantankerous and obnoxious to deal with. When God chose the metaphor of a shepherd to not only convey his role and nature, but also the role and nature of pastoral leadership, he chose an imagery that speaks of the sacrifice of and cost to the one who serves. But lest we forget, the calling to be a shepherd is ultimately a calling to be an under-shepherd where we live with the recognition that the flock ultimately belongs to Christ. He is the Chief Shepherd who holds us accountable for how we care for those assigned to us.

A Shepherd Suffers for the Flock

As with the first-century idea of being a slave, the concept of a shepherd begins with our understanding of Christ and his role within the church. In both the Old and New Testaments, the concept of a shepherd undergirded the coming of the Messiah and the nature of his activity. In Ezekiel 34:23–24, in response to the failure of the leaders of Israel to care for the people (vv. 1–10), God promises that he will send another shepherd and will set over the people one shepherd who will feed and care for them. He reiterates this again in 37:24 by promising that he will be of the lineage of David. However, in line with the genuine nature of a shepherd, this shepherd will ultimately lay down his life and be stricken on behalf of the people he serves (13:7–9; Zech. 11:7–14). However, the shepherd will suffer, not because he deserved his punishment because of any sin he committed (as was the case with the false shepherds), but for the benefit of the people that he cared for (12:10–13:1).

When Christ came, he boldly made the claim that he was the Good Shepherd, a claim that asserted that he was the messianic shepherd who came for his people. But he came not to rule over the sheep as a harsh shepherd, but as one who would lay down his life for the sheep. When Christ challenged Peter (John 21:15–17) and then Peter challenged the leadership of the church to be shepherds of God's flock (1 Peter 5:1–3), he challenged us to model our leadership and life after the same self-sacrificing character that marked Christ's service. Just as a slave can expect no better treatment than the master, so the undershepherd should expect no easier life than the Chief Shepherd. The reality is that the call to ministry is not just a call to suffer with and for Christ, it is a call to suffer on behalf of the church. Paul understood this when he stated in Colossians 1:24, "Now I rejoice in my sufferings for your sake." To understand the role of a shepherd is to understand that it intrinsically involves the willingness to suffer in order that the flock might be cared for.

A Shepherd Sacrifices for the Flock

The task of a shepherd begins with a willingness to sacrifice our personal comfort for the welfare of the sheep. In Jesus' parable of the lost sheep (Luke 15:1–7), the focus is often (and rightly so) upon the sheep and the love of the shepherd and his concern for the well-being of each individual sheep. But we cannot overlook the sacrifice the shepherd must make of his own comforts to go out and search for the lost sheep. Searching for a lost sheep means that the shepherd must go out in all kinds of weather and in the roughest and darkest regions of the pastureland. Sheep do not become lost in the open field but in the harsh areas where multiple dangers exist. When the shepherd leaves the ninety-nine in the open field, he does so at great peril and cost to his own safety. A shepherd unwilling to set aside his own welfare for the flock is not worthy to be a shepherd. God brought his indictment against the shepherds of Israel because they neglected to seek the lost sheep. Instead of risking being attacked by the beasts of the field, they remained safely at home, more concerned about their own welfare than that of the flock (Ezek. 34:1–8).

When we become more concerned about our own success, our own financial security, or our own comfort than we are about the needs of individual people in our congregation, then we are no longer worthy to be called shepherds. But this goes beyond just leaving the comforts of our office or home to go out and minister to the needs of people when we are tired and would rather be at home with the family. It means that we willingly suffer the attacks and criticisms of the very people we desire to serve. When dealing with sick animals, a shepherd must often risk the kicks and bites of the very animal that he is trying to help. A dog wags his tail and affectionately licks your hand when patting him on his head. But pry deeply to remove a painful thorn embedded in his paw and he will quickly bite.

Healthy Christians bring little trouble to a pastor. They encourage the pastor and recognize the role that God assigned them not only as leaders within the church but also as spiritual guides within their own life. They are not offended by any intrusion of the pastor because they recognize the pastor has been ordained by God to comfort in times of trials and confront in times of temptation and failure. However, it is the sick and the lost, not the healthy, that desperately need the true work of a shepherd. Without the activities of the shepherd, they are vulnerable to attack and death. Without the intervention of the shepherd, they would surely be lost. However, the sick and the lost often resent the intrusion of the pastor in their lives. Sin does not like to be uncovered, and it reacts to the probing of the one trying to reveal it. This is why being a pastor is inevitably a messy business. The very people who need us the most resent our intrusion the most. They react with criticism and personal attack to deflect attention from their own failures.

If we desire to remain in safety, more concerned about our comfort than their need, unwilling to be vulnerable to their personal assault, then we will quickly abandon them and turn our attention only to the healthy. But God condemns this attitude. In Ezekiel 34:1–6, God brings his indictment against the leadership of Israel because they were looking out for their own interests rather than the needs and interests of the flock. As a result, he removed them from being his shepherds (vv. 7–10). As Christ points out, the sick, not the well, desperately need the physician's touch (Mark 2:17; Matt. 9:12; Luke 5:31). But they often cause us the most problems. However, instead of striking back, we must continue to minister to them even in spite of our personal pain, for that is our calling.

For a pastor to sacrifice for the congregation he must be driven by his love for them. This love springs forth from his personal relationship with the sheep where the sheep know the voice of the shepherd and the shepherd knows the sheep (John 10:14). Yet the failure to care for the sheep and demonstrate a concern for those spiritually weak reveals an attitude that betrays a false shepherd. Zechariah takes it a step further by pointing out that God brings judgment upon rebellious people by providing them shepherds who do not "care for the perishing, seek the scattered, heal the broken, or sustain the one standing, but will devour the flesh of the fat sheep and tear off their hoofs" (Zech. 11:16). In other words, to those who refuse to walk in obedience, God, as an act of judgment, may give them shepherds who are more concerned about their own success and their own interests than they are the people. For these shepherds, people become merely a tool to be used, and ministry becomes a business where the bottom line of organizational growth determines success rather than the care and growth of each individual within the congregation.

A Shepherd Denies Himself for the Flock

A genuine shepherd willingly lays down his life for the sheep. In John 10:11 Christ sets forth the true measure of a shepherd when he states, "I am the good shepherd; the good shepherd lays down His life for the sheep." Ministry involves sacrifice and a willingness to place oneself at risk for the security of the sheep. This means that pastoral ministry is not safe; it is not a position for those who live in fear. The mark of a false shepherd is that they are unwilling to take any personal risks or face any sacrifice. Christ goes on to point out that a false shepherd quickly abandons the sheep when confronted with a threat to their personal safety, being more concerned about their own security than the protection of the flock (vv. 12–13).

As our society becomes more secular and more pagan, the cost of being a genuine shepherd of Christ increases. To remain true to Scripture, we risk being alienated and personally attacked. Where society once valued and highly respected the pastor in the community, such is no longer the case. To stand for the truth we expose ourselves to being labeled a bigot and closed-minded. We risk personal condemnation and denunciation. To uncompromisingly proclaim the truth opens us up to what others experienced before us: "Mockings and scourgings, yes, also chains and imprisonment. They were stoned, they were sawn in two, they were tempted, they were put to death with the sword; they went about in sheepskins, in goatskins, being destitute, afflicted, ill-treated" (Heb. 11:36–37).

A Shepherd Is Faithful to the Call

The final characteristic of a genuine shepherd is that he stands the test of time by remaining faithful in his service. In John 10:12, Christ warns that the hired hand, not a shepherd, quickly abandons the sheep when things get rough and threats appear. We serve the people willingly and freely, not for any benefit that we would receive in return (1 Peter 5:2–3; see also Luke 17:7–10), recognizing that our reward will come when Christ returns (1 Peter 5:4). We no longer serve to receive affirmation or financial gain. It no longer matters that they fail to understand everything we do, for we are serving Christ and it is he, not the congregation, who will give us our reward for our service. Yet, because we are undershepherds who must answer to the Chief Shepherd, we must recognize that God holds us accountable for his flock (5:2). The congregation does not belong to us. They belong to God; they are his property. What he requires from us is that we remain faithful in the administration of our duties.

WE ARE HUMAN

Perhaps one of the most difficult truths we face and have the most difficulty accepting is the reality that we are human. Pastor and author Wayne Cordeiro writes, "We don't forget that we are Christians. We forget that we are human, and that one oversight alone can debilitate the potential of our future."[18] We struggle with not only our own limitations as humans but also with the fact that we are indelibly flawed with the reality of our sin nature. Perhaps our greatest pain and struggle comes not from the external pressures we face, but the inward fear we feel because of our own sinfulness and frailties. Paul alludes to this when he writes in 2 Corinthians 7:5 of not only the outward afflictions

---

[18] Wayne Cordeiro, *Leading on Empty: Refilling Your Tank and Renewing Your Passion* (Minneapolis: Bethany, 2009), 13.

he faced, but also "fears within." In the grammar of the verse, Paul stress-es vividly that they constantly were lacking any relief from the troubles they were facing, troubles not only from external persecution, but also the internal apprehension we feel. This fear refers to the inward anxiety that Augustine describes as "mental perturbations."

Ministry can be depersonalizing. Because people look to you to provide answers to their problems, you can begin to deny that you yourself have questions left unanswered. You start to think that you are above the daily problems (marriage and family issues, financial strug-gles, temptations, etc.) that plague others. Being involved in the lives of many people can cause you to become relationally detached where you superficially interact with a number of people on a daily basis, but lack any in-depth relationship with anyone. Because people look to you as a spiritual leader, they begin to think that you are perfect and above all the struggles they face. But this dehumanizes a pastor, an elder, or any leader in the church.

Nevertheless, in the end we still remain human with all the warts and wrinkles of the soul that mar everyone else. Only by accepting our full humanity can we admit that we have needs and struggles. When we start to deny our discouragements, fears, struggles, and problems, we start down the road of emotional and psychological destruction. Rather than our weakness being a hindrance in ministry, it becomes the basis for effectiveness, since influence springs forth from authen-ticity. People are more receptive to our message when they see that we struggle with the same temptations and challenges they confront. Only by accepting our full humanity with all the emotional struggles and personal weaknesses can we begin to maintain a right perspective of ourselves.

Rediscovering Our Identity in Christ

But this all points us back to the very core of our identity: that your iden-tity must be in Christ, not in your ministry or in how others perceive you.

Tragically, we gain our identity and worth from our ministry and people's response to us, rather than our position and relationship with Christ. We forget that because of the work of Christ on the cross, each of us has "been crucified with Christ" and now say, "It is no longer I who live, but Christ lives in me; and the life which I now live in the flesh I live by faith in the Son of God, who loved me and gave Himself up for me" (Gal. 2:20).

Paul did not find the measure of his life in his accomplishments, but in his character and relationship with Christ. This defined him and served as the driving force in his service for Christ. We cannot base our self-worth upon the ministry, what we accomplish, the size and growth of the church, and the respect and treatment we receive from others. To do so will ultimately result in an identity crisis. People will fail and the ministry will have times of frustration and failure. Instead of looking for these things, we need to look to Christ. What is to define who we are is our character as it is transformed to conform to his character. When he defines our identity, then we are no longer driven by the circumstances we face, for our focus is not upon what we experience, but upon who we are in Christ.

In ministry we are wholly inadequate, completely flawed, and painfully sinful. All we can do is recognize that we are slaves and undershepherds who are not here to do our will or elevate our own prestige or fame. God calls us to continually point people to Christ and serve him in whatever capacity or position or circumstance he has placed us so that the glory might go to him and not ourselves. We are not the messiah given to the church; we are servants who serve the true Messiah by pointing people to him.

Yet even as we find clarity in our understanding of ourselves, our path once again becomes lost. If our life was only lived in the context of our relationship with God and our understanding of ourselves, then the path would be much easier to traverse. Just when we think we see the path clearly set before us, we turn the bend to find another entanglement. For our call is not just about living in a right relationship with God even in the midst of our suffering, but we are called to live in community. It is perhaps here in serving others that we find ourselves confronted with an impenetrable entanglement that prevents us from discovering genuine contentment in Christ.

6

Regaining a Perspective of Others

The Centrality of Love

The irony is striking, as it is tragic. We are called to a ministry devoted to loving and serving people and yet in the end we can become embittered towards the very people we serve. Some pastors remain in ministry but tragically have checked out in terms of ministering to people. They have become entrapped by their bitterness towards the congregation they shepherd.

What is the focus of our ministry? The question is not just an academic question of how we define ministry; it goes to the very heart of our perspective of people. As pastor Vern Wilkinson pointed out, "The reality is that people need to be at the center of our vision of ministry or the battle for right perspective is lost before the ministry begins."[1] The problem in ministry is that it can easily shift from being upon people to the organization of the church. Our attention shifts from people to running the programs, increasing the rolls, enhancing our own reputation, and recognition by our peers. When I first started ministry I remember hearing Howard Hendricks state, "There are only two things that God will take off this world—people and his Word, our job is to get his Word into people." But we can easily replace the eternal with the superficial. Instead of focusing upon the church as a community of individual people who make up the body of Christ, we focus upon the church as an organization. We lose clear perspective of the people we are called to serve.

---

[1] Vern Wilkinson, email message to author, November 2, 2014.

LOSING OUR PERSPECTIVE OF PEOPLE

Moses had enough. Time after time he responded with grace, compassion, and patience when the people brought their complaints before him. Even when God tested Moses' commitment to the people by threatening to destroy them, Moses responded with a plea for God to be patient. But in Numbers 11 his forbearance reached the breaking point. In verses 11–15 we find Moses lamenting his call to lead the people. The weight of leading over a million people through a desolate and barren wilderness overwhelmed him. When he came to the end of his lament, he cried out that death would be better than continuing to lead the people. The constant complaints of the people had distorted Moses' perspective. Like Moses, you can lose sight of God's work when you become focused on the grumbles of the people. Instead of seeing people as your calling, you see them as your cross to bear. When this happens you develop a distorted perspective.

Distortion Occurs When We Take People's Actions Personally

Previously when the people had brought their grievances to Moses, he had been able to remain detached from the grievances. But this time he took it to heart. Beginning in verse 1 of Numbers 11 we find once again the people complaining of the hardships in the desert. But this was no minor complaint; it constituted a rejection of God and as a result brought a consuming fire among them. After such a dramatic display of God's discipline one would think that it would have quieted the complaints. But it did not. In verse 4 they once again rose up and complained to Moses. They were tired of the manna that God provided and were threatening to turn back to Egypt. For Moses this was the final straw. In verse 11 he protests, "And why have I not found favor in Your sight, that You have laid the burden of all this people on me?" For Moses, the issue was no longer one of food, but an attack upon his leadership. It was personal. As a result he was ready to quit.

Being a pastor is more than just a vocation; it becomes your identity. It is not just what you do as a profession; it is who you are. Like Moses, when people find fault with your leadership or leave the church you take it as a personal rejection. Instead of caring about the people and their needs, we view them as a burden placed upon us. We start to resent their requests for help. We start to perform the minimum in ministry.

Distortion Occurs When We Have an Inaccurate View of Body Life

Just as people often develop unrealistic expectations of us, so also we fall into the same trap with people. We anticipate that they will be perfect saints who obey God without failure. We assume that they should be without fault or failure and that they should be mature believers. We often forget that spiritual maturity is a lifelong pursuit, having many ups and downs.

First, we develop faulty assumptions and expectations about people's involvement in the church. We wrongfully equate spiritual maturity with leadership. We assume that everyone should willingly serve as leaders and teachers in the church. What we fail to take into account is that people are gifted differently and have different functions within the church. Just because someone is not willing to teach a Sunday school class does not mean that they abrogate their responsibility to serve Christ and the church. While some have the gift of teaching, others serve in the areas of mercy and helps. In 1 Corinthians 12, Paul makes it clear that people have different roles within the church, and we need to be careful about making assumptions about what those roles should be. While many people exercise their gifts within the context of the ministry of the church, there are many others who utilize their gifts outside the realm of the church. For example, a person with the gift of mercy may help out at the local food bank rather than volunteer to help in the church. Whether some serve in the church as a teacher, others minister outside the church by meeting people's physical needs. Each act of service is critical to the health of the church. When we have a distorted idea that everyone should be willing to serve as leaders (due to the fact that we are always short of self-motived leaders), we start to become critical of people.

Second, we get a distorted view of people when we place unrealistic expectations of their commitment and passion for ministry. We often expect people to willingly give hours of their time each week to the ministry of the church. What we fail to recognize is that everyone has different demands upon their life. Some people have more time to give then others, depending upon their various obligations. For example, a person with young children may have less time to volunteer than a person who is retired. While everyone should be exercising his or her spiritual gift in some capacity, not everyone will be able spend the same amount of time and energy. Paul recognizes this point when he states, "The elders who rule well are to be considered worthy of double honor, especially those who work hard at preaching and teaching" (1 Tim. 5:17). While this verse points to the importance of recognizing those who give their lives full-time to the work of the church (as Paul and Timothy did), it also implies that there are many who are not able to do so. As a result, we should not dishonor or devalue their contribution. It may be that they are not spiritually ready for such a commitment. It may be that they are not able to give as much time because of their personal commitments.

Last, we often have unrealistic expectations of people's ministry skills. God uniquely equips every person both in giftedness and abilities. The parable of the faithful servant in Matthew 25 points out that people will have different talents. Just because one person is extremely gifted in teaching does not mean that all the teachers will share the same abilities. If we are not careful, we begin to become critical of others who are not as skilled as what we expect them to be. The parable of the talents points out that not everyone has the same abilities. We lament when others expect us to be able to preach as well as the gifted communicator on the radio, TV, or online, but we then turn around and place unreasonable demands upon them.

Distortion Occurs When We Leave Conflicts Unresolved

Conflicts are inevitable. Two people cannot exist very long together before some disagreement will arise. We will always have conflicts within the church because people have different opinions. However, the more personal the disagreement, the more intense the conflict will be. This is what makes conflicts so intense within the church. As pastors we deal with the core values of people. Through the preaching of the Word we are used by God to change the very identity of people from finding their identity in the world to having their identity in Christ. Consequently, when we confront people with their need to change, they will react with intense emotions. Being effective in ministry will always involve some degree of conflict. But the problem is not the conflict; the problem comes in our response. Do you respond with grace, forgiveness, and patience or do you react with anger and frustration? When conflicts continue without forgiveness and restoration, it colors your perception of people. You develop an adversarial attitude towards others. Instead of trusting people, you begin to question them. You look for ulterior motives and hidden agendas. Consequently, you become bitter towards people.

As a result of conflict we start to compromise our message. No one enjoys conflict. But the more we leave disagreements and hostilities unresolved, the more we will seek to avoid them. The end result is that we begin to avoid topics and issues that might cause people to react. We avoid culturally controversial issues even though Scripture clearly teaches about them. We preach to appease rather than transform. Instead of preaching to challenge people to live in obedience to Christ, we preach to make people happy and feel good about themselves.

Distortion Occurs When We Misunderstand Biblical Leadership

As we have already pointed out, we are called to be shepherds and slaves. The role that God has given us is to serve people, to sacrifice our own agenda for the well-being of others. However, the problem arises when we start viewing people as our servants. When this happens we start to see them as tools to use or mere employees who make us successful in our business. The result is that leadership is redefined. The focus shifts to program development rather than personal care. We become managers rather than shepherds where the focus is upon authority rather than service. The end result is that leadership becomes depersonalized. We become insulated from the people, preaching to audiences that have no personal relationship with anyone in the leadership of the church, or even in the membership of the church. We see people only as a number rather than real people facing ongoing spiritual struggles and in need of personal guidance. But this is not our calling. Success is not measured by organizational accomplishment but by personal and individual transformation. Paul understood this when he encouraged Timothy to "preach the word; be ready in season and out of season; reprove, rebuke, exhort, with great patience and instruction" (2 Tim. 4:2).

Symptoms of a Distorted View

The distorted view that we have of people has enormous implications for ministry. Since our ministry is with people, any distortion that we have will affect how we serve them. As we look at the church today, we can see the effects. The pastoral role has become a pathway to recognition rather than self-abasement. Success is defined by numbers and the size of the church rather than faithfulness and obedience.

Authoritarian Leadership

Recently a church made national news as it imploded because of the inward conflicts between the pastoral staff. However, a closer look revealed a glaring absence of anyone from the congregation serving as elders. Somewhere in the formation of the church there developed a lack of trust for the laity that led to authoritarian leadership. This points to a deeper problem than our philosophy of church leadership and our ecclesiology. It points to a distorted view of people that leads to a distrust in the involvement of the laity. Instead of recruiting them for leadership, we circumvent them. Because we no longer trust them, we develop an authoritarian style of leadership where all the decisions are regulated to a select few rather than the congregation. Professors and former pastors Roger Heuser and the late Norman Shawchuck describe the effect that this has upon the organization: "Suspicion is everywhere. Reality is categorized into 'good' and 'bad' and 'us' versus 'them.' The organization is characterized by hostility and insecurity. Problems are distorted and magnified. Since suspicious leaders are extreme controllers, those who are hired and promoted will usually reflect and promote the leader's own views. Within such a climate of distrust, the atmosphere is often depressive."[2] When this becomes the characteristic of the leadership the ministry becomes dysfunctional, as the pastor is more concerned about controlling than serving.

Lack of Bonding between the Congregation and Pastor

When the pastor's perspective of the people becomes tainted, the pastor is no longer able to bond with the congregation. The congregation views the pastor as an outsider instead of accepting him as a part of the fellowship. The pastor, instead of integrating himself into the lives of the people and earning the trust of the people, presumes some authority as an outside expert. As we pointed out in chapter 1, the church suffers from short-term pastorates. While there are a number of reasons for this, certainly a distorted perspective of people is a significant contributor. Pastors become frustrated with the congregation and leave to go to another church in hopes of finding people more passionate about ministry. Instead of bonding where there is mutual love and commitment, there is distance and superficial relationships. Pastor David Hansen describes the importance of the bond between the pastor and

---

[2] Norman Shawchuck and Roger Heuser, *Leading the Congregation: Caring for Yourself While Serving Others* (Nashville: Abingdon, 1993), 101.

the congregation when he writes, "When a church and a pastor do not bond, the church cannot grow—in numbers, in commitment to one another and to God, to mission, to worship, and to a deeper spirituality. The simple reason is that all growth involves change and risk, which causes most individuals and all congregations profound anxiety and threatens to keep us from taking the steps to growth."[3]

For this bonding to occur, not only must the congregation learn to trust the pastor, but the pastor must also learn to trust the people. If there is not this mutual trust, then the pastor will only remain a few years (or until the honeymoon period is over), and then move on in search of greener pastures. But this lack of trust in the people goes deeper than just a pastor's distorted view of the congregation; it also reveals a lack of trust in God—that he works through each individual within the congregation by his Spirit to accomplish his purpose. The end result is that the church learns to view the pastor as an outsider who comes as a hired gun for a short time before riding on to the next town. This clergy-laity distinction undermines the priesthood of all believers where the whole congregation functions as servants within the church, exercising their gifts for the growth of the fellowship.

Breakdown of Teamwork

The work of ministry is the work of the whole church working together to advance the kingdom of God. However, for the leadership and the people to work together as a team in ministry there must be mutual trust. Leadership and management expert John Maxwell highlights the importance of teamwork when he states, "A good team is always greater than the sum of its parts, but teams of leaders increase their effectiveness exponentially."[4] Without an effective team, the church will only

---

[3] David Hansen, *The Power of Loving Your Church* (Minneapolis: Bethany, 1998), 61.

[4] John C. Maxwell, *Developing the Leaders Around You* (Nashville: Thomas Nelson, 1995), 137.

be able to accomplish what the pastor can do. But if we have a distorted view of people, then we will never entrust others to both make decisions in ministry and actively pursue ministry. Throughout the pages of Scripture we find over and over again that God calls all people to be involved in ministry. It is not the work of the pastor or the board. The role of the leadership is to equip the congregation to do the work of ministry (Eph. 4:11–12). But this can only be accomplished when there is mutual respect, trust, and support in ministry, all of which is at the heart of teamwork. This begins with the pastor having a healthy view of the rest of the congregation.

This brings us back to trust—a trust in both the people you serve and in the God who is at work. When you no longer have confidence in people, you no longer delegate in ministry. Instead of allowing others to serve and equipping them to serve, you start to do all the work yourself. You do not trust those who serve alongside whether fellow pastors, ministry leaders, or the congregation to make wise decisions. We do not respect our board to guide us and provide oversight for our ministry. We do everything in the church ourselves because we can do it better. The end result is we become burned out and the people become complacent. In the end everyone loses.

RESTORING OUR PERSPECTIVE

You cannot remain effective in ministry without a right perspective of people. Ministry is not about running an organization, it is not merely conveying truth, and it is not developing programs. Ministry is people. Having a clear perspective of people is not only necessary for longevity in the church; it is foundational for effectiveness.

Effective Ministry Requires a Right Attitude about People

Village Missions, an organization focusing upon "Keeping the Country Church Alive," has as its central theme that it seeks to engrain in all its pastors: "Preach the Word, Love the People." In this motto they touch upon the core of what biblical ministry requires in terms of one's approach to leadership. As a pastor we must do more than just love the church; we must also love each person within the church and community. Love, rather than the pursuit of success, must be the driving force behind every action. Hansen summarizes the scope and demands of such love: "Pastors cannot do pastoral work for people they hate or even dislike. Love is our life's work. We must love our church in order to do our job. The process of pastoral work for persons and churches we dislike or even hate is to learn to love those persons and churches."[5]

This love is more than warm feelings of affections; it is a deep commitment that places the best interests of others above your own regardless of how they respond or treat you in return. It is genuine *agape* love that characterized Christ's love for his bride. We often use Ephesians 5:22–33 to preach on marriage. In presenting the passage we use Christ's love for his bride to be an illustration of the type of love a husband is to have for his wife.

But if we look closer we find that in reality Paul is reversing it. Rather than use Christ and the church to illustrate marriage, he uses marriage to illustrate Christ's love for the church. In verse 32 he makes it clear that the main point he is making is related to Christ and the church. This brings up a critical point in a shepherd's attitude towards the church: Do you love the church as much as Christ does? Or to use the illustration Paul does in his appeal to husbands, do you love the church as much as you love your wife? Too often we abandon the church in search of a more appealing "lover" (a more prestigious church with higher pay and greater recognition). We reveal a lack of faithfulness to the ministry in which God has placed us. Is it no wonder that so many people "church hop" when that is the model we as pastoral leaders ourselves have presented to them? This is not to say that we should never leave a particular church to move on to a different one. There are times when God moves us in a different direction. But it must be for the right

---

5   Hansen, *Power of Loving Your Church*, 106.

reasons. Moving or staying must be based on God's will for our ministry and what is best for the churches we serve, not just because we have an opportunity to move up the ecclesiastical ladder.

While much debate has centered on the terms for love used during the interaction between Peter and Christ in John 21:15–17, we cannot miss the central point. To serve as an effective shepherd one must be governed and driven by a deep love for Christ and for the people. It is this love that enables us to look beyond their faults, beyond the offenses, beyond the callousness, beyond the sacrifices, and beyond the pain. The amount of pain we are willing to suffer for someone reveals the amount of love we have for that person. Christ points this out when we states, "Greater love has no one than this, that one lay down his life for his friends" (John 15:13). This is the standard that he places upon us (15:12, 17). He further clarifies the extent of this love when he states that we are not just to love our friends, but also our enemies (Matt. 5:44). While we affirm these truths from the pulpit, we find it far more difficult to affirm them in our daily life. Instead of loving people in our congregation who cause us pain, we become bitter and resentful. In so doing we nullify our ministry.

To love the people means that we are willing to sacrifice for them. The depth of love is not measured by what we do, but by what we are willing to sacrifice. We see the depth of Paul's love when he states, "For I could wish that I myself were accursed, separated from Christ for the sake of my brethren, my kinsmen according to the flesh" (Rom. 9:3). Paul loved the people so much he was willing give up his own salvation if it would bring about the redemption of others. This seemed to be irrational, the prayer of a crazed fanatic.[6] But this was the proof of his

---

[6]   Heinrich August Wilhelm Meyer, *Critical and Exegetical Hand-book to the Epistle to the Romans*, trans. from 5th ed. of the German John C. Moore (chaps. 1–8) and Edwin Johnson (chaps. 9–16), trans. rev. and ed. William P. Dickson, with a preface and supplementary notes to the American ed. Timothy Dwight, Meyer's Commentary on the New Testament 5 (1884; repr., Peabody, MA: Hendrickson, 1983), 358.

love, a love that had its roots in the love of Christ who likewise was will to become a curse for us for our salvation (Gal. 3:13; 2 Cor. 5:21).

Few of us would make such a request. Yet this is the same prayer that Moses prayed when the nation of Israel rebelled against God by turning to idolatry. In the face of the threat of God's judgment against Israel, Moses offered himself: "But now, if You will, forgive their sin— and if not, please blot me out from Your book which You have written!" (Exod. 32:32). What the church desperately needs today is not more eloquent preachers or great visionaries, but pastors who would forfeit everything, including their salvation (if that were possible) for the benefit of the people they serve.

If you love people, you will be affected deeply by the struggles they face, whether the struggles are in their personal life or in their relationship with Christ. Paul did not rebuke the church at Corinth to vindicate his ministry and defend his reputation. He was moved to write because of his deep love for them, a love that led him to weep even as he penned the letter: "For out of much affliction and anguish of heart I wrote to you with many tears; not so that you would be made sorrowful, but that you might know the love which I have especially for you" (2 Cor. 2:4). Where we might have become angry because of the personal attacks, Paul wept! This is the heart of a leader. A leader weeps for his people.

We Are Called to Minister to People Not Just Organizations

When we approach ministry we often focus upon the organizational nature of the church. We focus upon overseeing the ministries, planning the events, and staffing the programs. Often this encompasses a significant portion of our weekly activities. But this is not the heart of our calling. We are not called to care only for the organization of the church; we are called to care for the people of the church. While we must oversee the programs of the church and while we may not know everyone in the church (depending on the size of the congregation), we must never lose sight that ministry is ultimately about relationships rather than programs. When Christ reinstated Peter to ministry after his disastrous failure, he did not say, "Peter, develop programs for the church" or "Peter, have a clear vision for the church." He said, "Peter, feed my sheep." This rivets our focus not upon the church as an organization, but the church as a community of individuals who are in desperate need of spiritual care.

We cannot state it enough: the ministry is people. When we think of the church we often focus upon the building, the organization, the programs, and the duties we perform as pastors. What we need to remember is that the ministry is about people. The organization is merely the means to the end, not the end itself. Nevertheless, we are drawn to the organizational function of ministry because it is easier. Visions, program development, and strategic planning are controllable and can be clearly defined. People are more difficult. Working with people requires ministry without all the answers. It is perplexing and challenging. It requires flexibility and adaptability. It leads us into the realm where we constantly confront our own inadequacies and failures.

We Must Maintain a Right Attitude about the Spiritual War

A battlefield remains not only dangerous, but confusing. It is not always clear whose side the combatants are on. In guerrilla warfare the enemy easily assimilates into the crowd. The result is that the ability to clearly identify the enemy becomes drastically hindered. The fog of war often results in unintended casualties due to friendly fire. The same is true in the spiritual war. When we face struggles and trials in ministry, often we can attribute the problems to the actions of people. As a result we begin to see people as the enemy. But Paul reminds us that our "struggle is not against flesh and blood, but against the rulers, against the powers, against the world forces of this darkness, against the spiritual forces of wickedness in the heavenly places" (Eph. 6:12).

We are engaged in a spiritual war where the enemy uses people as tools, pawns, or human shields. Christian leaders need to remember that our adversary is Satan and the battle is for the very people inflicting the most pain upon us. It was this perspective that enabled Jesus to pray, "Father, forgive them; for they do not know what they are doing" (Luke 23:34). Stephen likewise also prayed even as the Jews were stoning him, "Lord, do not hold this sin against them!" (Acts 7:60). Both Stephen and Jesus recognized that the Jews who were attacking them were not the enemy. Their human antagonists were in fact prisoners of war—slaves whom the enemy had captured to do his will (2 Tim. 2:26).

Because "our struggle is not against flesh and blood" (Eph. 6:12), we must offer people who oppose us grace rather than judgment. We must see beyond the hurt they cause and see that Satan has "blinded the minds of the unbelieving so that they might not see the light of the gospel of the glory of Christ, who is the image of God" (2 Cor. 4:4). Is this easy? No, but it helps to remember that people and their eternal destinies are the focal point of the battle. In this conflict into which our Master calls us to do battle as his slaves against our true enemy (Eph. 6:10–18), we do not fight for territory or resources (as is often the case of human conflicts in history) but for the spiritual destiny of people (Matt. 25:46; John 3:36). When people personally and wrongfully attack us, it serves to remind us that the enemy has captured them, and God calls us to minister as slaves of Christ to bring them freedom (John 8:31–32; Rom. 1:16–17; 2 Cor. 10:3–5).

But not only must we recognize our enemy, we must also recognize our fellow soldiers in the battle. In the pressures and struggles of ministry we start to think that we stand alone and isolated against the enemy. Like Elijah we can start to think that we alone are left to fight the battle (1 Kings 19:10). But we are not alone, for God still has his people proclaiming his message. God's plan is never thwarted and his message is never silenced. There are people who are always preaching the gospel. God has an army of people. But this army is not just the other pastors who labor alongside of us. Our co-workers are the whole church. People in the church, even those who sometimes hurt us, are still our co-workers serving the King alongside of us.

God Uses Crooked Sticks to Draw Straight Lines

It is easy to express appreciation for those who support and encourage us as we serve. But how do we respond to those within the church who cause us problems? It is one thing when people outside the church oppose you. It is quite another when those who criticize you are fellow workers in the cause of Christ. In Philippians 1:12–14, it does not surprise us that Paul would express his joy and appreciation for those who were supporting him in his imprisonment. When we are going through trials, we desperately need and appreciate those who stand by our side. However, it is what he says next that perplexes us. He goes on to express his joy even for those who were seeking to undermine his ministry by promoting their own agenda (vv. 15–17). These were not the false teachers that Paul later warned about in chapter 3. These were people who were a part of the church but were proclaiming the gospel with the eye for their own recognition and self-promotion. Surprisingly, Paul does not condemn them. Instead, he focuses upon the fact that even though they may not have the right motive, as long as they had the right message he saw that they still had value in the ministry. There were two reasons he could have this perspective.

First, unlike these pretentious preachers, Paul's only concern was for the gospel to be preached. For this goal he was willing to set aside his own personal reputation. Even though these individuals refused to serve Paul, they still were serving the advancement of the gospel. Like Paul, their self-interest was subordinated to the gospel, and so in this he still rejoiced. By pointing this out Paul also brings clarity to the Christians in Philippi where divisions threatened the unity of the church (4:2). New Testament scholar G. Walter Hansen describes Paul's perspective in this situation: "By telling of his response to the envious preachers, Paul lets the church in Philippi know that the negative attitudes of some toward him in the church are of little or no importance. He minimizes the significance of disputes caused by his personality, his position, and his prestige. As long as the gospel advances, his promotion or demotion does not matter to him."[7] Keeping the promotion of the gospel rather than ourselves as the focus enables us to keep others in perspective.

Second, Paul understood that God uses fallen people with all their weaknesses and personal failures to advance his kingdom. He can draw a straight line with a crooked stick. Even if their motives were not entirely righteousness, the fact that they preached the gospel meant that God could still use them. This is not to say that Paul was not concerned about their motives; by mentioning them he brings a subtle rebuke. But Paul also recognized that God can use even flawed and immature people to advance his kingdom, and because of this he could still rejoice in their work and still value their contribution to the kingdom (4:18).

In the church you will have people who support your ministry and prove to be your constant allies. There will also be individuals who, because of their immaturity and sin, pursue their own interests and agenda. They will support only their own programs and undermine others that might threaten their position. Nevertheless, even though they may be acting in inappropriate ways, they can still be used by God to advance his kingdom, and so we can still rejoice in their efforts. But this also serves as a reminder of our own failures and self-serving motives. In many ways we are no different from them. Paul understood this. Even as he mentioned the improper motives of these individuals, he recognized his own. Like them, he too was a crooked stick, marred by sin and still in pursuit of righteousness (3:12–14). The same could be said for each one of us.

We Need to Be Willing to Be Vulnerable

Our natural tendency when attacked is to withdraw and put a protective guard around us. We avoid close friendships in order that our weakness might not be exposed and used against us. It does not take long in

---

[7]   G. Walter Hansen, *The Letter to the Philippians*, Pillar New Testament Commentary (Grand Rapids: Eerdmans; Nottingham, England: Apollos, 2009), 75–76.

ministry to become guarded in relationships. The first time someone uses our own admission of shortcomings against us we start to build a protective wall to conceal our inward struggles. When I was first in ministry, I remember hearing older pastors warn against developing close relationships with people in the church. They had been hurt too many times.

Astonishingly Paul did just the opposite. Instead of being guarded and protective, he became even more open, honest, and vulnerable. The church at Corinth was a dysfunctional church. Even though Paul invested almost two years of his ministry in the establishment of this church, it continued to struggle. A quick perusal of the two letters he wrote to them reveals a deeply troubled church. They tolerated blatant sin in their midst. Infighting and division marred them. Their doctrinal beliefs bordered on heresy. The marriages in the congregation were in shambles. Even their worship became corrupted by gluttony, misuse of tongues, and disorderly confusion. To top it all off, they criticized Paul's abilities, questioned his apostolic authority, and maligned his character. It must have pained Paul greatly for he had invested a significant amount of time and energy in seeking to establish this church. Rather than become bitter towards those who attacked him, he continued to demonstrate patience and compassion.

It would have been natural for Paul to become very cautious when he dealt with the church. Yet, what is shocking to us as we read the letters of Paul, it was before this church that Paul revealed his inward struggles and fears. Rather than becoming restrained in disclosing any of his struggles, he became even more transparent:

Paul admitted that he came to them in weakness and much fear (1 Cor. 2:1–5).
He confessed that he was the least of the apostles (1 Cor. 15:9–10).
He described his great affliction and suffering, being burdened beyond his strength and despairing of death (2 Cor. 1:4–8).
He revealed how much he was burdened for them (2 Cor. 2:4).
He mentioned that he felt inadequate for ministry (2 Cor. 3:5).

He referred to himself as a clay jar, easily broken, and described all the struggles he faced in ministry (2 Cor. 4:7–18).

He expressed the deep fears he felt and the depression he struggled with (2 Cor. 7:5–6).

He readily admitted that he was "unskilled in speech" even though they had been critical of his speaking abilities (2 Cor. 11:6; 10:1, 10).

He acknowledged his need of humility and his personal weaknesses (2 Cor. 12:7).

Paul did not reveal his weaknesses to manipulate them into feeling sorry for him. Rather, it was to point the Corinthian believers to the surpassing greatness of God's grace. Paul understood that people who attack and criticize others are people who fail to understand God's grace.

When people nitpick and readily point out our failures, they are not rejecting us; they are rejecting the necessity of grace both in our lives and in theirs. Those who criticize others often do so in order to elevate themselves. Paul's answer was to show the bankruptcy of all. By being more open with his own shortcomings, he provided the foundation for addressing their spiritual problems. Paul did not want to give them the impression that he was playing their game, pointing out the faults of others in order to deflect attention off his own. Instead, by revealing his own struggles he gave greater authority to his message of God's mercy. In the end, we are all in the same boat—sinners in desperate need of God's grace. Rather than becoming guarded and protective, we need to be more open and honest about our own shortcomings, even when people may use those confessions against us. By doing so we further highlight the depth and wonder of grace—grace that God bestowed upon us and that we are to demonstrate to others.

We Are to Serve Regardless of Response

We are all familiar with the story of Jesus healing the ten lepers in Luke 17:11–19. There was no greater tragedy to befall a person than to contract leprosy. To be a leper was to experience horrific physical suffering. Yet the physical effects paled in comparison to the emotional and psychological trauma of becoming an outcast as a result, shunned by society and alienated from family and friends. For them to experience the miraculous healing of Christ would have brought relief from the worst nightmare. Therefore it is both shocking and tragic that only one of them would have taken the time to express gratitude to Jesus and glory to God for the healing he experienced. What is even more surprising is that it was the one person we would least expect to give glory to the God of Israel: a Samaritan. Yet as a result of this simple act of faith, this person not only experienced physical healing but spiritual healing as well. When Jesus said to him, "Stand up and go; your faith has made you well," the implications go far beyond his physical healing.

As we read the story we often overlook an important question: Why did Jesus heal the other nine? Before he healed all ten, he knew that only one would respond in faith. The other nine were merely using Jesus as a tool to achieve their own agenda. Jesus could have easily denounced the nine for their selfishness and healed only the Samaritan. Nevertheless, he still healed them even in spite of their rejection of him. But this attitude of Jesus—healing and ministering to people who would still reject him—was characteristic of his ministry. While there were many who did accept the messiahship of Jesus because of his healing touch, there were others who responded with indifference. Matthew's Gospel records that Jesus had compassion on the multitudes and healed all their sick (14:14). Yet at his trial there was no one who stood by his side to express support. Even those who were healed by Jesus abandoned him and joined the crowds in demanding his death. In another instance, Jesus healed the soldier whose ear was cut off by Peter even though he was coming to arrest him. Even today we see Jesus miraculously intervening in the lives of people to protect them from tragedy, yet they attribute it to Lady Luck.

But this brings us to the point we need to remember regarding our own ministry. We are to serve people regardless of their response. In ministry we derive a sense of significance and accomplishment by how people respond to us. When people fail to respond positively, when numerical growth does not happen, when there are no tangible results, we become discouraged and resentful. What we fail to recognize is that our calling is to serve Christ regardless of the results. What Paul states in general is especially true for pastors: "Whatever you do in word or deed, do all in the name of the Lord Jesus, giving thanks through Him to God the Father. . . . Whatever you do, do your work heartily, as for the Lord rather than for men, knowing that from the Lord you will receive the reward of the inheritance. It is the Lord Christ whom you serve" (Col. 3:17, 23–24).

When you base your ministry upon the response of people rather than the service of Christ, you have lost perspective. There will be times when you pour your time and energies into the lives of people and have nothing to show for it in the end. But this does not mean that you have failed. Just the opposite. The very act of your obedience, where you follow the example of Christ by being faithful regardless of the response, is the greatest achievement you can accomplish.

The People Belong to Christ

When Jesus reinstated Peter, he did not say, "Feed *the* sheep." Instead, he said, "Feed *my* sheep." In this simple statement he made it clear that the people we serve ultimately belong to Christ, and he is the one responsible for them. In the high priestly prayer recorded in John 17, Jesus likewise affirms this: "I ask on their behalf; I do not ask on behalf of the world, but of those whom You have given Me; for they are yours; and all things that are Mine are Yours, and Yours are Mine; and I have been glorified in them" (vv. 9–10). While we affirm this truth, we often overlook the implications it has for us.

First, because the people and the church belong to Christ, ultimately he is responsible for the spiritual health of the congregation. One of the reasons we become distorted in our view of people is because we have a distorted perspective of what our ministry is. While it is certainly true that we are responsible to proclaim truth accurately and oversee the spiritual health of the congregation, it is equally true that ultimately Christ is responsible for the condition of the church. Our task is to be obedient to Jesus and his leadership. Paul understood this when he stated, "What then is Apollos? And what is Paul? Servants through whom you believed, even as the Lord gave opportunity to each one. I planted, Apollos watered, but God was causing the growth. So then neither the one who plants nor the one who waters is anything, but God who causes the growth" (1 Cor. 3:5–7).

This is not the confession of a fatalist who believed "whatever would be would be" so that he never took responsibility for his ministry. Rather, it was the confession of one who understood his position in Christ and the role that God had given him. He understood that the bottom line was not what he achieved, but how obedient he had been to Christ. This is what enabled him to maintain his passion and love for a church that continually criticized him. He summarized this in the next chapter when he stated, "Let a man regard us in this manner, as servants of Christ and stewards of the mysteries of God. In this case, moreover, it is required of stewards that one be found trustworthy. But to me it is a very small thing that I may be examined by you, or by any human court; in fact, I do not even examine myself. For I am conscious of nothing against myself, yet I am not by this acquitted; but the one who examines me is the Lord" (4:1–4).

This perspective brings accountability in ministry as well as freedom. This gives us freedom from the pressures of success so often plaguing pastors and causing us to become discouraged. We are not controlled by man's standard of success, but God's; a standard that is grounded upon faithfulness and obedience rather than achievement and recognition. But it also brings accountability, for we are accountable to God for how we lead. While he is responsible for the health of the church, he will hold us responsible if we lead the church away from him (Heb. 13:17; James 3:1).

Second, because the people belong to Christ, he has the right to arrange the church and the people as he desires. Growing up on the farm we would select certain cattle to move to a different pasture. Often the cattle resisted the change and would want to go back to the herd, or those who were left would try and follow the ones being moved. Not once did we ever ask the cattle if that is what they wanted. The same is true of Jesus as the shepherd. We often take it personal when people leave our church to go to another. Nevertheless, we need to recognize that sometimes Christ rearranges the sheep according to his sovereignty. Certainly if someone is leaving because of sin and a desire to flee accountability in church discipline, we should confront the person. But often people leave a church because it no longer is a "good fit" for them. It is not that they are angry with us; it is just that God may be "moving them to a different pasture." When this happens we can still rejoice and trust a sovereign God and focus on those whom he has given to us.

We Serve People Attacked by Wolves

In Matthew 9:36 we find a glimpse into the heart of Jesus and his assessment of people, a viewpoint that we must maintain in order to effectively serve the church. At the beginning of the chapter we find Jesus ministering in his home region around Nazareth. It was a region where he was both praised and vilified. While some praised his healing powers, others accused him of blasphemy. Even when he brought deliverance to a demon-possessed man, the people attributed it to the power of Satan rather than the power of God.

Many in Jesus' position would have easily become frustrated and angry at the fickleness of the people. But Jesus had a different perspective, which we see revealed in verse 36: "Seeing the people, he felt compassion for them, because they were distressed and dispirited like sheep without a shepherd." The descriptive terms "distressed" and "dispirited" are both graphic and powerful in the image they present. The former pictures an animal lying wounded with its skin flayed and torn by the ravenous attacks of wild beasts; the latter describes one who is thrown down with a mortal wound. This does not refer to the physical illness and misery of the people, but rather the spiritual condition of their lives. New Testament scholar Donald A. Hagner describes their condition this way: "What causes Jesus' deep compassion at this point is not the abundance of sickness he has seen but rather the great spiritual need of the people, whose lives have no center, whose existence seems aimless, whose experience is one of futility."[8] This was why Jesus was moved deeply within his soul, for he saw the spiritual bankruptcy of the world in which he lived. This same world we live in today.

The statement that they are "like sheep without a shepherd" brings to mind that Jesus is the Chief Shepherd, he is the answer. But here the text takes a surprising turn. Rather than then expound upon himself being the shepherd, he turned to the disciples and commissioned them to be his workers in the midst of a ripening field (Matt. 9:37–38). In ministry we must see both the needs of the people as well as Jesus' answer. The people we serve are distressed and dispirited, and Christ, the Lord of the harvest, has sent us to bring hope to them. It is both this vision of people's brokenness and our realization that we are commissioned by God that must motivate us to serve the congregation.

Remaining Thankful for the People We Serve

Grumbling people can create complaining pastors. Not so with Paul. No matter how difficult the church and challenging the problems needing correction, Paul almost always expressed genuine thankfulness for the people. Even for the church at Corinth, which caused him so much trouble, he still thanked his "God always concerning you for the grace of God which was given you in Christ Jesus" (1 Cor. 1:4). This brings us to the heart of our attitude towards people. When we our perception of the people becomes distorted, we become critical rather than thankful. Instead of rejoicing in their salvation, we complain of their shortcomings.

Paul did not look at the church through rose-colored glasses that blinded him to their spiritual faults. He was both honest and realistic in

---

[8] Donald A. Hagner, *Matthew 1–13*, Word Biblical Commentary 33A (Dallas: Word Books, 1993), 260.

his assessment of the churches. Nevertheless, he did view them through the lens of God's redemptive work. For all their problems (and there was often many) he still saw them as the work of God and the recipients of grace. Furthermore, he did not see himself alone as righteous while they were plagued with immaturity. Rather, he saw himself at one with them in their weaknesses and struggles. To be effective in ministry we need to learn to be truly thankful in ministry. We can be thankful for all people in the congregation regardless of how they treat us because we have a God who is working, a God who is able to soften the hardened heart, a God who bestows grace upon the broken, a God who cares deeply for each individual within the congregation.

All this brings us back to our love for people. We cannot provide the sacrificial care for people that Jesus desires if we do not love them. Jesus continually stressed that as the shepherd he loved his sheep, and it was this love that motivated him to lay down his life for them. The same must be true for us. However, you must carefully guard your heart and attitude lest you become cold and distant from the people you serve. When ministry becomes the most challenging, you must continually be reminded that the call to serve is a call to love. Daily we must pray that God will stir his love in us.

In 2 Corinthians 5:14 Paul summarizes the motivation for his appeal to people with the gospel, "For the love of Christ controls us, having concluded this, that one died for all, therefore all died." The genitive "of Christ" can be understood as either subjective (i.e., Christ's love for us) or objective (i.e., the love we have for Christ). Perhaps it is best to understand that both are in view, for they are not mutually exclusive. If we understand the depth of Christ's love for us, it will lead inevitably to a deep love for Christ (Luke 7:47; Rom. 5:8). But it doesn't stop there, for it also has implications for our view of others. To love God and his Son is to love people (1 John 4:7–11). It is this love that enables us to look beyond the hurt that people cause us and see the spiritual needs they have (Rom. 5:5). When we love people as Christ loved us, then we can continue to serve people through the most difficult circumstances and struggles.

Tragically it is in the service of others that we find our greatest struggles. Instead of ministry being a blessing, it becomes a curse. Too often many have come to the end of the journey exhausted and burned out, finding that the path they trod has ultimately brought them to a worn-out, bitter end. Was this our calling? Is this what God intends for our life? I think not. Before we reach that end we must recognize that there is one more signpost pointing us in a different direction.

7

Regaining a Perspective of Ministry

You started ministry enjoying the calling given by God to those who shepherd his flock. You enjoyed communicating God's Word each week. You fell in love with the people. Every week you rejoiced that God would enable you to give your life to the very thing you love.

With time, however, the struggles mount and the discouragements continue such that ministry soon moves from a joy-filled activity to little more than a duty thrust upon you. You begin to see ministry as merely a task to perform rather than also a privilege and calling from God. While Paul saw ministry as a gift graciously given to him (Eph. 3:7), when going through trials in ministry you begin to wonder if it is a curse. You soon lose the joy of ministry. You become apprehensive every time the phone rings and someone asks to meet with you. You approach meetings with foreboding and dread. Visitation becomes an obligation. Even preaching, which should be the high point of ministry, becomes a weekly obligation. When you preach, you feel like Sisyphus in Greek mythology, cursed to roll a large boulder up a hill only to watch it roll down again. You preach with a sense of futility rather than empowerment and accomplishment.

But is that God's intent? Did he call you to do something where there is no joy in the task? Are you to begrudgingly go about the day "suffering for Jesus" with the hope that you will only experience the joy of Christ in the eschatological future?

To maintain our perspective in the midst of the trials of ministry, we must recognize that not only is life a gift from God, but ministry itself is a gift God has given us to enjoy. We need to learn to see the pleasure of ministry and to recognize that God takes pleasure in blessing us, although not always in the way that we think. We must learn to enjoy God's gift, not by finding freedom from difficulties, but in the midst of them.

LIFE IS A GIFT OF GOD TO BE ENJOYED

The book of Ecclesiastes has often been maligned as a book espousing man's wisdom apart from God. However, such an approach not only does injustice to the biblical text, but it does a grave injustice to the book itself. If the sole purpose of Ecclesiastes is to provide us with the highest of uninspired reasoning of the natural man, there are plenty of places we can find such information. As Anglican theologian J. Stafford Wright summarizes, "It does not seem to be worthy of God to occupy a valuable space in the Bible with arguments of a skeptic and the natural man. We can buy those anywhere or have them for nothing."[1]

The writer of Ecclesiastes points us not to the skeptic and natural man, but to all the incongruities of life and the search for meaning that continually seems to be thwarted by the apparent failures, struggles, and tragedies we face. But this directs us to find our purpose in God. Only in a relationship with God can one discover the true understanding of life. The opening section of Ecclesiastes sets this up, as Old Testament scholar Walter C. Kaiser Jr. explains: "Life in and of itself, even God's good world with all its good, God-given gifts, is unable to deliver meaning and joy when it is appropriated in a piecemeal fashion. This . . .

---

[1] J. Stafford Wright, "The Interpretation of Ecclesiastes," in *Classical Evangelical Essays in Old Testament Interpretation*, ed. Walter C. Kaiser Jr. (Grand Rapids: Baker, 1972), 137.

is the meaning of the prologue: 'Vanity of vanities, all is vanity': namely, that no single part of God's good world can unlock the meaning to life. Life, in and of itself, is unable to supply the key to the questions of identity, meaning, purpose, value, enjoyment, and destiny. Only in coming to know God can one begin to find answers to these questions."[2] In our relationship with God we find the basis for joy and happiness rather than in the circumstances and events and accomplishments of this life.

This begins with the understanding that life is to be enjoyed regardless of the external events that happen in our life. For the writer of Ecclesiastes, life can only be enjoyed in the context of our relationship with God, and he masterfully weaves this theme throughout the fabric of the whole book. At every turn, after pointing out the paradoxes of a fallen world, he brings us back to this thesis (3:3; 5:18–20; 8:15; 9:7–9; 11:8–9; 12:13–14). He continually reminds us that "there is nothing better for a man than to eat and drink and tell himself that his labor is good" (2:24; cf. 3:12–13, 22; 5:18–19; 8:15; 9:7–9). Some might conclude that the writer is a hedonist or an Epicurean sensualist who espouses the philosophy "let us eat, drink and be merry, for tomorrow we die."

But this would contradict the very theme and conclusion governing the book: "Fear God and keep his commandments" (12:13–14). For the sage, only in the context of our relationship with God can we find the true basis for fully enjoying the life God has given us. God, and only God, gives true meaning and understanding in life, for in the end every pursuit apart from God merely tries to grasp a vaporless cloud (i.e., vanity of vanities, all is vanity), one seen but lacking any true substance.

Thus Wright rightfully sums up the point that the writer drives home:

> "Vanity of Vanities, all is vanity." "Fear God, keep his commandments . . . God shall bring every work into judgment." The first is a verdict on all life. The second is counsel in view of the verdict. But is the verdict true? That is what Koheleth [the Preacher] examines for us, turning life over

---

[2]   Walter C. Kaiser Jr., *Ecclesiastes: Total Life* (Chicago: Moody, 1979), 17.

and over in his hands so that we see it from every angle. And he forces us to admit that it is vanity, emptiness, futility; yet not in the sense that it is not worth living. Koheleth's use of the term "vanity" describes something vastly greater than that. All life is vanity in this sense, that it is unable to give us the key to itself. The book is the record of a search for the key to life. It is an endeavor to give a meaning to life, to see it as a whole. And there is no key under the sun. Life has lost the key to itself. "Vanity of vanities, all is vanity." If you want the key you must go to the locksmith who made the lock. "*God holds the key of all unknown.*" And he will not give it to you. Since then you cannot get the key, you must trust the locksmith to open the doors.[3]

We live in a fallen world, where sin corrupted the enjoyment of the life God gave. But instead of shrinking back in discouragement and fatalistic despair, we recognize that even though broken by sin, God still gives us life as a gift to be enjoyed. Old Testament scholar Duane A. Garrett emphasizes this perspective in terms of the importance of receiving God's gift of life and its attendant joys:

> The Teacher tells his readers how to live in the world as it really is instead of living in a world of false hope. In short, *Ecclesiastes urges its readers to recognize that they are mortal.* They must abandon all illusions of self-importance, face death and life squarely, and accept with fear and trembling their dependence on God. . . . Life should be enjoyed for what it is—a gift of God. The book counsels that while avoiding the temptation to consider pleasures to the point of being the goal of life, one should not miss the fleeting joys life affords.[4]

Whereas Job confronts the paradox of faith by challenging us to let God be God, Ecclesiastes confronts the paradox of faith by challenging us to enjoy life as a gift of God with all its incongruities. This enjoyment

---

[3] Wright, "Interpretation of Ecclesiastes," 140.

[4] Duane A. Garrett, *Proverbs, Ecclesiastes, Song of Songs*, New American Commentary 14 (Nashville: Broadman & Holman, 1993), 278.

comes, not by denying the reality of life's pains, but by looking beyond them to see that meaning comes from our relationship with God rather than external circumstances.

In Hebrews 12:2 we read: "Jesus, the author and perfecter of faith, who for the joy set before Him endured the cross, despising the shame, and has sat down at the right hand of the throne of God." While we find Christ experiencing deep anguish as he faced the horrors of the cross, he did so with joy, not because of the joy of the cross, but because of the joy of what the cross achieved. When we place our focus upon God and his work through us, then we have joy even in the midst of the suffering we face. Not because we find joy in the suffering itself, but we find joy in the fact that God uses us to achieve his eternal plan. Suffering and affliction result in shortsightedness. We become fixated with the present and the circumstances we face. But Scripture points us to be farsighted, to become focused not on the present with its problems, but with the eternal and its triumph.

We Find Joy in Ministry Because of Our Identity in Christ

Gaining a correct understanding of ministry begins with our identification with Christ. When Saul of Tarsus encountered and submitted to the person of the risen Jesus on the road to Damascus, it brought a radical change in his identity (Acts 9). Not only was his name changed to Paul, but also his whole persona was transformed. He was not only a believer and beneficiary of the redemptive death and resurrection of Christ, but a recipient of the character and nature of Christ, imparted to him so now he said, "It is no longer I who live, but Christ lives in me" (Gal. 2:20). Because of his identification with Christ the world then directed their hatred of Christ towards Paul. Consequently, as we have already seen, Paul did not see his suffering and pain in ministry as a mark of shame and repudiation; rather, he saw his scars as a badge of honor, demonstrating his identification and relationship with Christ.

But the rest of the apostles shared this same view. In 1 Peter 4:13–16, Peter expressed the same view when he wrote, "But to the degree that you share the sufferings of Christ, keep on rejoicing, so that also at the revelation of His glory you may rejoice with exultation. If you are reviled for the name of Christ, you are blessed, because the Spirit of glory and of God rests on you. Make sure that none of you suffers as a murderer, or thief, or evildoer, or a troublesome meddler; but if anyone suffers as a Christian, he is not to be ashamed, but is to glorify God in this name." This points to the certainty of suffering for all Christians. If the world hates Christians, how much more will they hate those who serve as leaders?

When we enter ministry, suffering is unavoidable and inescapable. Mistakenly, we think that we should be exempt from suffering. For a minister of Christ to say that he should not suffer is equivalent to a fish saying he does not like to swim in water. Both are the inherent consequences of their true identity. Rather than leading us to despair, it should cause us joy, for our suffering reveals our true identification with Christ. While we do not rejoice *for* our suffering, we can rejoice *in* our suffering, for our suffering testifies of our position in Christ. As followers and servants of Jesus, we have been granted the greatest privilege of all God's created universe; not only do we have the imprint of his image as descendants of Adam, but we have the character of Christ instilled within us as his spiritual descendants. By God's grace we became co-heirs with him, gaining the privilege of inheriting all the honor and position of being a genuine son of the Father.

This future reward places the present difficulties we face in perspective. Our suffering is temporary; our inheritance is eternal. Our position as the object of ridicule is replaced by the shared honor of a son. Our present trials serve as a precursor to our future glory (Rom. 8:18). When we experience times of difficulties, we often feel abandoned by God and we wonder if God's promises remain true. However, rather than our sufferings being an indication that God has abandoned us, they serve as an affirmation of our union with Christ. Consequently, we can rejoice, not because of the sufferings themselves, but because they reveal our nature and position in Christ (2 Tim. 3:12). For just as his promise is true that we will suffer for Christ, so also it is true that we will be rewarded by participating in his glory (Matt. 5:10–12; 2 Cor. 4:16–17).

We Rejoice in Ministry Because of the Privilege of Serving

When we encounter trials and difficulties, ministry can soon become a burden. Instead of the joy, we wonder if ministry is a curse that we must endure. However, for the apostles, the call to ministry was the greatest privilege that could be given. It is not an accident that the writers of the New Testament refer to the service of God as a gift. But the word "gift" is more than something given without cost. Paul uses the same word to both describe the incredible gift of our salvation (Rom. 6:23) and to describe the spiritual gifts we have received to serve him (Rom. 12:6; 1 Cor. 12:28). In contrast to a wage which someone gives based upon the merit of the recipient, a person gives a gift freely, and it demonstrates the benevolence and loving character of the giver. Concerning this gift of salvation, New Testament scholar David Brown rightfully summarizes,

> But "eternal life" is in no sense or degree the wages of our righteousness; we do nothing whatever to earn or become entitled to it, and never can: it is therefore, in the most absolute sense, "the gift of God." Grace reigns in the bestowal of it in every case, and that "in Jesus Christ our Lord," as the righteous Channel of it. In view of this, who that hath tasted that the Lord is gracious can refrain from saying, "Unto Him that loved us, and washed us from our sins in His own blood, and hath made us kings and priests unto God and His Father, to Him be glory and dominion for ever and ever. Amen!" (Rev. 1:5, 6).[5]

When we think of the unparalleled demonstrations of God's infinite grace we most often (and rightfully so) refer back to our salvation. But no less a demonstration of his infinite benevolence is the call

---

[5]   Robert Jamieson, A. R. Fausset, and David Brown, *Commentary Critical and Explanatory on the Whole Bible* (1871; Oak Harbor, WA: Logos Research Systems, 1997), 2:236, comments on Romans 6:23 by David Brown.

and privilege to serve the living God of the universe. We easily become discouraged if we do not receive any positive affirmation or encouragement. But we do not find the joy of ministry in the response of the people we serve, but in the privilege of serving the one who called us. *Serving God is its own reward.* We continually rejoice because God has bestowed upon us the honor of serving him. What greater favor can be bestowed than serving the living God on a daily basis? There is no greater privilege than serving Christ and his people with our time, talents, and spiritual gifts. As pastors, we have the privilege of being the vessels that God uses to communicate his life-giving message to a dying world. We have the privilege of representing and communicating his love letter to people.

The world in which we live is broken, seriously and irreversibly broken. Sin corrupts and destroys all that lies in its clutches. It devastates relationships, dreams, countries, and individuals. It seeks to annihilate all that it touches. We live in a world "separate from Christ, excluded from the commonwealth of Israel, and strangers to the covenants of promise, having no hope and without God in the world" (Eph. 2:12). This truth we affirm in our theology but often fail to recognize in the daily lives of the people with whom we come in contact. We easily lose sight of the fallen, broken lives of people. The report of a mass murder or rapist reminds us of the depravity of man, but we often fail to see it in our next door neighbor who demonstrates many of the qualities of a Christian but never really embracing the unconditional salvation that Christ offers. While we theologically affirm that salvation is never attained through personal effort or inherent goodness, there is a part of us that secretly believes we should still try to earn it. This undermines the recognition of the privilege and importance of ministry. If good people get to heaven, then there is no longer the need for a preacher (except perhaps in prison where evil people are sent). Our calling loses its value.

However, when we see that all people exist hopeless without Christ, no matter how good and moral, then our ministry becomes of eternal importance. Apart from the hope of salvation, people confront an eternity in hell. In response to the lostness and brokenness of humanity, God not only sent his Son to provide the means of salvation, but he graciously sends us to provide the message of salvation. Paul reminds us of this in Romans 10:13–15, "For 'whoever will call on the name of the Lord will be saved.' How then will they call on Him in whom they have not believed? How will they believe in Him whom they have not heard? And how will they hear without a preacher? How will they preach unless they are sent? Just as it is written, 'How beautiful are the feet of those who bring good news of good things!'"

This is your calling—that God has chosen you to be among those sent by the living God to bring his message to lost and broken people. There is no other occupation like it in all the world. You have the privilege of affecting the lives of people for all eternity. How could we ever become disillusioned in ministry? How could we ever shrink back from the calling and become angry with God for calling us to this task? The gift of being a pastor-teacher, along with every gift given to the church, is priceless. God has given us a great privilege —the task of being his vessels through whom he communicates his salvation.

There was a period in my ministry when I stepped down from being a pastor and served as the director for the Center for Leadership Development for Village Missions. When I told my father that I was resigning from being a pastor, his comment was, "I am disappointed." For him there was no greater job than being a pastor. While he may have not have fully understood the value of every gift and that the exercise of a gift could be expressed in a number of different ways, in some ways he was right! If I was called to be a pastor, I could do nothing better.

But with great privilege comes great responsibility and great opposition. If our calling is so great, then we can expect that there will be opposition and personal attacks. This comes with the territory. The fact remains that not only do we remain in a broken world, we enter a spiritual battle where Satan desires to destroy any and all the works of God. Where God's grace is most evident, Satan's opposition will be most pointed. So we should not expect to escape the onslaught of his attacks.

Rather than becoming disillusioned in ministry, adversity serves as a continual reminder of the greatness of our responsibility.

We Rejoice in Ministry Because of the Sufficiency of Christ

As we go about our daily tasks, we must remember that Christ personally empowers us. Not just that Christ watches over us and even injects his protective hand from time to time, but that Christ actively equips us to achieve his work. When Paul evaluated his own ministry, not only did he see the eternal significance of it and the importance of his all-out effort, but he saw that everything he did was done through the empowerment of Christ rather than his own strength (Col. 1:28–29). It is easy and inevitable to become discouraged if we look only at ourselves—our abilities, our talents, our wisdom, and our strength. But Paul reminds us that our sufficiency is not in ourselves but in Christ who empowers us.

First, he is sufficient to empower us to effectively accomplish his eternal purpose. This becomes the basis for our confidence as well as our assurance that our ministry will be effectual. We are not called to a task that we are ill-equipped to perform. Through Christ, we possess everything necessary to accomplish his purpose for our life and ministry even if we fail to see the results (2 Peter 1:3). But therein lies the problem. Discouragement plagues us because we often do not see what our efforts accomplish. You compare yourself to others who appear to be "successful" and you see yourself as coming up short. Other pastors are better communicators, better organizers, more dynamic, more gifted, clearer visionaries, stronger exegetes, and the list goes on.

When you start to compare yourself to others, you soon wonder if the church would be better served by a different pastor. It is not the Moses who led the people of Israel that we identify with, but the Moses who cried out, "Please, Lord, I have never been eloquent, neither recently nor in time past, nor since You have spoken to Your servant; for I am slow of speech and slow of tongue" (Exod. 4:10). Even after God reminded Moses that he had equipped him for the task set before him (vv. 11–12),

Moses still saw himself as unfit, crying out, "Please, Lord, now send the message by whomever You will" (v. 13). What Moses needed to learn (and each of us also) is that the sufficiency for ministry comes not from ourselves, but from the empowerment of the living God. You can be confident in ministry, not because of your intrinsic talents and abilities, but because of the living God who both calls you and equips you. Your competence is found in Christ, not yourself; it is his work, not yours.

Second, because of his enablement and grace, we can experience God's blessing upon our ministry. We constantly feel inadequate, not only because we feel ill-equipped, but also because we feel wholly unworthy of the task. So we fall into the trap of trying to earn the blessing of God upon our life and church. We desire nothing more than this. But it always seems so elusive. While pursuing and seeking his blessing, we are never sure we ever attain it. This is especially true when our ministry seems to be floundering in the realm of stagnation, when attendance decreases and programs are getting nowhere, when people continually struggle with the same old problems and remain unchanged by our most powerful sermons. Sometimes we cry "Ichabod," wondering if the glory of God has departed from our ministry. Accordingly, we equate God's blessing with our worthiness and efforts. This then robs us of our joy. We continue to serve, but we feel forgotten and forsaken by God.

Rediscovering your joy in ministry is not found in the attainment of success but rather in the reaffirmation of the sufficiency of Christ's grace. You are competent in ministry because his grace is sufficient, and his empowerment is abundant. Because of the grace of Christ, not only do you no longer need to earn God's salvation, you no longer need to earn his blessing upon your life and ministry. Just as you can never earn salvation, you can never earn God's blessing. Rather, he freely gives it because of the work of Christ on the cross.

We Rejoice Because of the Growth of Others

The problem we face is that we cannot readily see results to measure our effectiveness. The results that we seek to obtain are spiritual not physical. How do you place a quantitative measurement upon the spiritual growth of people? You look at numbers in the pews, but measuring success by numbers can be deceptive. A large following does not necessarily indicate inward transformation. It can and it may, but bigger is not necessarily better when it comes to the ministry of the church, especially in America. Measuring genuine spiritual transformation can be elusive. At times, an individual will manifest a radical, life-altering change, but in most cases the growth comes gradually and incrementally.

Imagine standing before a newly planted tree. For the first several years, we see rapid growth; but after a number of years, the tree seems to stop growing. In the first few years, we could measure the height of tree and measure the growth by feet. But as the years go by, the rapid upward growth slows and even seems to stop. Year after year we look at the tree and see little, if any, growth. However, reality often differs from perception. What we perceive to be the periods of little growth is actually when the tree grows the most. The greatest growth in the volume of board feet comes when the tree becomes so large it no longer appears to be growing.

So it is with the spiritual growth of people. When a person first experiences the redemption of Christ, the transformation is both dramatic and highly visible. But as time goes on, it seems as though people become stagnant with little growth occurring. However, what we fail to realize is that God is still at work within the individual. God works in the inward motives and character of the individual in ways not always clearly seen (Heb. 4:12). We easily see the power of God at work when a person gives up a bad habit, but the real power of God works inwardly to teach a person to love the unlovely and forgive the unforgivable. The outward habits and lifestyle are far more visible than the inward qualities of joy, forgiveness, and peace. Yet these are the areas that God is most at work. The best way to see the growth of a tree is not by standing and watching it grow, but by comparing the sapling with the old growth timber. It is only then that we see the full extent of the growth.

As pastors we are tree watchers. Every day we watch the tree that does not seem to grow. Year after year the tree appears to be the same.

Yet every year a new growth ring appears, testifying of substantial, although seemingly invisible growth. Like a timber grower, we cannot control the growth of the tree, but we can make sure that the right environment exists to make growth both favorable and inevitable. Only God can orchestrate the growth in the lives of individuals; however, he uses us to create the right environment to assure that growth. Philippians 1:6 assures us that growth inevitably occurs: "He who began a good work in you will perfect it until the day of Christ Jesus."

Christ points us to the mystery of spiritual growth when he teaches the parable of the seed in Mark 4:26–29: "The kingdom of God is like a man who casts seed upon the soil; and he goes to bed at night and gets up by day, and the seed sprouts and grows—how, he himself does not know. The soil produces crops by itself; first the blade, then the head, then the mature grain in the head. But when the crop permits, he immediately puts in the sickle, because the harvest has come." The growth of the gospel is inevitable, not because of what we do, but because of the intrinsic nature of the gospel itself (1 Peter 1:23).

My father, a man who learned the lessons of life in the wheat fields of Idaho, once said, "You do not have to change to be accepted by Christ, but if you accept him you will change." He knew the laws of farming. You cannot cause a plant to grow, but if you create the right environment, the plant will grow. So it is also in Christ. The environment for growth is found in the pages of Scripture. This is why Paul boldly stated, "I am not ashamed of the gospel, for it is the power of God for salvation to everyone who believes" (Rom. 1:16). Growth and change will happen because the Holy Spirit is constantly creating the right environment through the proclamation of the Scriptures. When we create the environment for growth by our preaching, then growth will happen in the lives of people even if it is not readily visible to the eye. To see it, we must look closely and deeply.

The problem is that the trials and struggles of ministry create shortsightedness where we see only the problems rather than the triumphs of grace. But if we look beyond the problems, we will discover that spiritual growth happens. We do not find our joy in the numerical growth of the church and the increase of programs and facilities. It is not found by moving up the church corporate ladder by pastoring larger and larger churches so that eventually we gain recognition by our peers. Rather, our joy comes in the spiritual growth of people, in the unity of the church, and the healing of relationships (Phil. 2:2). We experience joy when people live their life daily in obedience to Christ (Rom. 16:19) and walk in the truth (2 John 4; 3 John 3). Over and over again the apostles stated that their joy in ministry was not found in the success of the church's programs or even size of the congregation, but in the people themselves (Phil. 4:1; 1 Thess. 2:19–10). We do not find true joy when programs are well attended and people stroke our egos with praise. Instead, we experience genuine joy when one individual comes to a saving knowledge of Christ (Luke 15:7), when the people we serve demonstrate "good discipline and the stability of [their] faith in Christ" (Col. 2:5).

The reason we often lack satisfaction in ministry is because we look for the wrong thing. We seek to find affirmation of our "success" rather than the transformation of one individual. We become discouraged because we focus upon those absent rather than those present. When we get up on Sunday, we become discouraged if the attendance is down rather than rejoicing for those who come desiring to know God and hear what God has to say to them. Our happiness is not to be found in masses but in individuals growing in Christ. It should cause us joy when we see one person transformed. God did not call you to ministry only to have you leave it discouraged and disheartened. He called you to ministry that should bring unparalleled joy, for you have been given the front-row seat of watching him demonstrate his love and value for each individual by working personally in their lives so that they reflect him.

We Rejoice in the Proclamation of the Truth

We must ask ourselves this critical question: "What brings us the most pleasure?" As we have already pointed out, most often we answer the question based upon personal affirmation and ministry success. Those events and accomplishments that serve to affirm our value and worth bring us joy. We experience greater personal satisfaction when people appreciate our efforts and our activities accomplish significant results. Let's be honest, Monday morning is always brighter if our attendance was up on Sunday and people were complimentary. While these are nice, the problem is that these things are not always present. However, when we look at the early apostles, the basis for their joy differed radically from ours. We find our joy in what we accomplish in ministry; they found their joy in the ministry itself. We find our joy in the results of service; they found their joy in the act of service. The difference is enormous.

The reason we often struggle to find joy is that we base our joy on what we cannot control. No matter how hard we work, how many programs we dream up, how many hours we spend in the church, how well prepared and dynamic our messages, in the end these cannot guarantee our "success." God's sovereign work, not our efforts, determines the results our ministry achieves. We need to look no further than the prophets of the Old Testament who were called only to be "failures" in their mission. For example, Isaiah was not called to lead the people in great revival, but to confirm their judgment by revealing their hardheartedness (6:8–13). It is no wonder that he cried out, "Lord, how long?" (v. 11). Ironically, Israel's most successful prophet became angry with God when his ministry and preaching led to a national revival within the capital city of an archenemy (Jonah 4).

One of the marks of genuine Christian love is the joy that comes when the truth of God's word is revealed. Thus Paul writes in the love chapter that love "does not rejoice in unrighteousness, but rejoices with the truth" (1 Cor. 13:6). This comes from one who was deeply familiar with failure, rejection, and the personal pain that comes with doing ministry. However, these were not the focus of Paul's attention. His focus was upon the gospel. For Paul the greatest joy was found in the proclamation of Christ.

If we truly believe that Scripture is the inspired Word of God and that Christ is the only answer to a sinful world, then there should be no greater joy then the opportunity to share that message with others. While we should always rejoice when people respond to the truth, we should never lose the joy that comes in the proclamation of the truth. Each week, and at other times throughout the week, we have the privilege of communicating the truth of God to people. Whether they respond or not should never diminish this honor afforded to us. There is joy even if they reject the truth, for even by proclaiming it to them, we have both given them the opportunity to respond and vindicated the justice of God—namely, that no one is without excuse, and God is always just in his judgment. In the preaching of the truth, we affirm that a prophet has been among them and in so doing we fulfill our calling and responsibility (Ezek. 2:5; 3:1–21; cf. 1 Cor. 14:24–25). God did not call us to organize and develop programs. He called us to faithfully communicate his love letter to people. Consequently, every time you proclaim God's Word, you can rejoice both in the fact that the truth has been revealed as well as in the fact that you have fulfilled your calling as a pastor and teacher.

We Rejoice in Ministry Because of the Rewards That Await

The joke is as old as it is corny: "The pastor's salary is not great, but the benefits are out of this world." But how many times do we stop and reflect upon the truth of the statement. While we focus upon the meagerness of the salary, we often overlook the importance of the last part of the joke—that we will be rewarded for the ministry we perform. We naturally focus on the present with all its struggles and problems. We see all the circumstances and events that rob us of our present happiness. We focus upon the board member who undermines our leadership. We become discouraged because all our efforts to start a new program to reach the community seem to accomplish little. We become obsessed by the lack of attendance. We lament the lack of denominational support and encouragement, especially when they continue to praise those who experience numerical growth, thus implying that this should be true of every church. While they do not expressly state it, we feel the pressure that if our church is not growing, somehow it is our fault.

But in the midst of this, Scripture constantly points us in a different direction. Instead of focusing upon the immediate, it challenges us to focus upon the eternal. The immediate is both temporary and deceptive. Success is always fleeting. Praise soon becomes criticism. Even in ministry, we pursue the present joys only to find continual troubles. In response, Paul reminds us to look elsewhere, to see eternity and then view the present through that lens (2 Cor. 4:1–18). When we look at the problems of the day, they soon become overwhelming: "we are afflicted in every way, but not crushed; perplexed, but not despairing; persecuted, but not forsaken; struck down, but not destroyed; always carrying about in the body the dying of Jesus, so that the life of Jesus also may be manifested in our body" (vv. 8–10). Truly did Jesus say, "Each day has enough trouble of its own" (Matt. 6:34). But when we focus on eternity, all the issues we encounter soon begin to pale by comparison.

Through the apostle who knew labor and hardship beyond what most of us have ever experienced or imagined, God challenges us in Scripture not to look at eternity in light of the present, but to look at the present in light of eternity: "For momentary, light affliction is producing for us an eternal weight of glory far beyond all comparison, while we look not at the things which are seen, but at the things which are not seen; for the things which are seen are temporal, but the things which are not seen are eternal" (vv. 17–18). This is especially true in ministry. If we find our joys in the present rewards then we will be sorely disappointed. So we must look elsewhere, to the rewards that we gain in heaven.

In the parable of the talents (Matt. 25:14–30), Jesus takes the spotlight off our talents and onto the joy of serving. While the parable is familiar, the lessons need to be continually pressed home even to those who preach it most often. Jesus emphasizes the importance of faithfulness in service rather than the outward achievements. While the first two individuals where given different amounts, and they achieved different results, the reward was the same. As New Testament scholar D. A. Carson points out, "Different amounts (though all very large) were given to each servant, *according to his ability*, and the return expected was in proportion to the sum entrusted. God recognizes that we are all different and expects of us only what is appropriate. It is significant that the two successful servants receive identical commendations from the master (vv. 21, 23), even though the scale of their original responsibility, and therefore of their achievement, is different."[6]

The master did not condemn the last servant because he failed to measure up to the achievements of the other two. He condemned that servant because he hid the talent rather than faithfully used it for the benefit of the master (vv. 26–30). While we often make the servant's faithfulness the focus of the story, we should not miss that the story also highlights the reward that each received. The statement "enter into the joy of your master" is an imperative that implies both the immediacy of the act and a personal response to the command. But the joy that is here referred to here is not the joy that we experience in the present, but the joy we shall share with the Father in the age to come.

Seeing beyond the present to eternity and the joy we will experience in heaven provides the foundation for our joy now. No matter what we encounter in ministry, no matter how devastating the circumstances, no matter how tragic the trials, our eternity and reward remains assured. As a result, Peter challenges us to "greatly rejoice with joy inexpressible and full of glory" even when going through present trials of various kinds (1 Peter 1:3–9). The crisis we face in the present never threatens the eternal rewards already reserved in heaven for us. This inheritance, that we are co-heirs with Christ, is protected, not by our ability, but by the power of God. If our focus shifts to the current trials, then we no longer will have any joy. But if our focus remains upon eternity, than we can rejoice no matter what we face.

Ministry will always have its ups and downs. There will be times when your ministry seems to be blossoming. There will be times when it seems as though it withers on the vine. There will be times when

---

[6] D. A. Carson, R. T. France, J. A. Motyer, and G. J. Wenham, eds., *New Bible Commentary: 21st Century Edition*, 4th ed. (Downers Grove, IL: InterVarsity Press, 1994), comments on Matthew 25:14–30.

you are excited about what God is doing in the church, and there will be times when it seems as if God is absent. There will be times when people praise you for your ministry, and there will be times when you are confronted with harsh and unjust criticism. But in all the ups and downs of ministry nothing changes the reality that our reward is already attained. The present does not define our ministry or its success; our eternal reward, which is based upon faithfulness, defines the success and significance of our ministry.

So often in ministry we become focused upon the negatives rather than the benefits. We hear the criticisms rather than the compliments. We become discouraged by those who leave the church rather than be encouraged by those who demonstrate substantial growth. We remember the failures and easily forget the triumphs. There will always be issues and problems that cause us to be discouraged. But if these become our focal point, then we will lose perspective. We cannot (and should not) deny the problems and challenges, but we must never lose sight of the joys as well. When we focus upon the joy of serving Christ and his church, then we can have the perspective of Christ who "for the joy set before Him endured the cross, despising the shame, and has sat down at the right hand of the throne of God. For consider Him who has endured such hostility by sinners against Himself, so that you will not grow weary and lose heart" (Heb. 12:2–3).

Conclusion

Our journey has brought us at last to the central key to maintaining a right perspective of suffering, of ourselves, of others, and even of ministry itself. The key is found in the enjoyment of God. At every turn, the answer to maintaining our perspective is found in looking to God and keeping our focus upon him. He is the Alpha and the Omega, the beginning and the end, not just of history, but life itself. Christ points us to this in his high priestly prayer: "Father, the hour has come; glorify Your Son, that the Son may glorify You, even as You gave Him authority over all flesh, that to all whom You have given Him, He may give eternal life. This is eternal life, that they may know You, the only true God, and Jesus Christ whom You have sent" (John 17:1–3). Our salvation is not just about deliverance from the clutches of hell; it is about entering into a personal relationship with the living God. The joy of ministry is found in seeing God and his activity clearly. When you find yourself discouraged, disheartened, feeling unappreciated and ineffective, it serves as an indication that you have lost your focus. Your focus is no longer on Christ; it has drifted to yourself, to others, or to your circumstances.

God did not give us this ministry to torment us as if somehow it becomes our ecclesiastical penance. He gave us this ministry as the greatest privilege he bestows upon a human being. The greatest gift we could ever receive is that the living God would not only redeem us from our sin, but call us to be his ambassadors of reconciliation to the world. Yes, your call involves a call to suffering, to trials, to self-denial. But it should never be viewed as a burden. Trials and discouragements—yes; despair and bitterness—never. The ministry has been given to us to enjoy, not just to enjoy God as we gain a better understanding of his sustaining care, but to enjoy all aspects of serving him.

In Christ we enjoy the people, enjoy the preaching, enjoy the development of programs, and even enjoy the trials. In Christ we find joy in the ebb and flow of ministry, the accomplishments and the defeats, the days of plenty and the days of want. There is nothing like it in all the world. There is no job or career that is more privileged and more rewarding than to be a servant of the living God. We enjoy the ministry not because we enjoy the trials, but because we enjoy the God who calls us and sustains us, the God who placed us in this position as one of the greatest gifts that can be given. We enjoy the ministry because we know that God has already secured our eternity and these present trials are not a threat to our relationship with him (Rom. 8:34–39). The struggles we face in the present are only temporary, earning for us a far greater reward that shall not fade or diminish.

As shepherds, we will weep. But in the midst of our weeping we must keep the right perspective about ourselves, about God, about others, and about our calling. The moment we lose perspective, we already begin to abandon ministry. The reason Paul could endure all the pain, tears, and trials was not because he was superhuman or a supersaint, but because he never lost his perspective. At the end of his life, as Paul passed the baton of ministry on to the next generation, he challenged Timothy to keep his perspective when he wrote, "Remember Jesus Christ, risen from the dead, descendant of David, according to my gospel, for which I suffer hardship even to imprisonment as a criminal; but the word of God is not imprisoned. For this reason I endure all things for the sake of those who are chosen, so that they also may obtain the salvation which is in Christ Jesus and with it eternal glory. It is a trustworthy statement: For if we died with Him, we will also live with Him; If we endure, we will also reign with Him" (2 Tim. 2:8–12).

This perspective enabled Paul to face his approaching execution with confidence: "For I am already being poured out as a drink offering, and the time of my departure has come. I have fought the good fight, I have finished the course, I have kept the faith; in the future there is laid up for me the crown of righteousness, which the Lord, the righteous Judge, will award to me on that day; and not only to me, but also to all who have loved His appearing" (2 Tim. 4: 6–8). May our prayer be the prayer that A. W. Tozer penned near the end of his ministry: "Pray for me in light of the pressures of our times. Pray that I will not just come to a wearied end—an exhausted, tired old preacher interested only in hunting a place to roost. Pray that I will be willing to let my Christian experience and Christian standards cost me something right down to the last gasp!"[1] May we not just start ministry well, but may we finish with our hands still on the plow, testifying of his grace no matter the cost. For a time we may weep, but in the end our weeping will be turned to laughter and our sorrow into joy.

> I will extol you, O Lord, for you have lifted me up,
>> And have not let my enemies rejoice over me.
> O Lord my God,
>> I cried to You for Help, and You healed me.
> O Lord, You have brought up my soul from Sheol;
>> You have kept me alive,
>> that I would not go down to the pit.
> Sing praise to the Lord, you His godly ones,
>> and give thanks to His holy name.
> For His anger is but for a moment,
>> His favor is for a lifetime;
>> Weeping may last for the night,
>> But a shout of joy comes in the morning.
>
> Now as for me, I said in my prosperity,
>> "I will never be moved."
> O Lord, by Your favor You have made my mountain
>> to stand strong;
>> You hid Your face, I was dismayed.

---

[1] A. W. Tozer, *The Pursuit of God*, ed. James L. Snyder (1948; repr., Ventura, CA: Regal, 2013), 135.

> To You, O LORD, I called,
>> and to the Lord I made supplication:
> "What profit is there in my blood, if I go down to the pit?
>> Will the dust praise You? Will it declare Your faithfulness?
>
> "Hear, O LORD, and be gracious to me;
>> O LORD, be my helper."
> You have turned for me my mourning into dancing;
>> You have loosed my sackcloth
>> and girded me with gladness,
> That my soul may sing praise to You and not be silent.
>> O LORD my God,
>> I will give thanks to You forever. (Psalm 30)

In the journey of our human experience there are not one but two times we weep. We weep when we encounter pain and sorrow, when we stand alone and rejected, when we feel there no longer seems to be any hope. The other occasion we weep is radically different; it is the time when we weep for joy, when we experience the exhilaration of having all our longings and desires meet, when we realize the pain is gone and joy has come.

To be a shepherd is to be called to a life of weeping. There will be times when we weep because of the pain we experience. There will be times when we weep for the pain of the people we serve. But there will also be a time when our weeping in sorrow turns to the weeping of joy. This will come when we stand before the Chief Shepherd and we hear the words that we have so long desired to be spoken, "Well done, thou good and faithful servant." It is then that we will realize that in all our struggles we were not alone, but we were constantly empowered by Christ to fully accomplish his will and purpose. Once again we will weep, but now we will be shepherds who weep for joy. It is when we learn to have this as our perspective what we will have learned to be content in whatever circumstance we face.

Glenn C. Daman grew up on a farm in Tensed, Idaho where he attended a small rural church. He attended Big Sky Bible College, Western Seminary, and Trinity Evangelical Divinity School. Since 1991 Glenn has served as the pastor of River Christian Church in Stevenson, Washington. He has also served as the director of Village Missions' Center for Leadership Development and has been an adjunct professor for a number of Bible colleges and seminaries in the area of small-church studies and has taught in Russia, the Philippines, Canada, and Mexico. Glenn is the author of *Leading the Small Church, Shepherding the Small Church,* and *Developing Leaders for the Small Church.* He enjoys woodworking and photography as well as going back and working on the farm where he grew up. Glenn also enjoys spending time with his wife and best friend, Becky, as well as their children and their families.

Printed in the United States
By Bookmasters